How This Book Will Help You

This book is a great read if you are a manager or a supervisor; even if it is only being in charge temporarily for a day.

Author, Deborah L. Whitworth, has been a human resource manager for over 20 years. She has seen it all! She believes that management isn't rocket science but a process, where the manager acts as a good role model. She teaches by example and tries to do everything right.

Deborah believes that management is not an exact science. It is an art form. Some of us happen to be born with more talent than others. She claims that not everyone is management material and if so, you should admit it, accept it and move on.

You want to do the right thing. Unfortunately, nobody has told you what the right thing is. In this book, Deborah will help you determine if you are management material, or not, or whether you need a little help. She'll act as a role model and show you *how to manage yourself, so you can be free to manager others*.

Deborah shares some memories from her past experiences, as human resources manager in a variety of industries. She realises that practicing good management doesn't come easy to all managers. *The goal of this book is to provide you with a step-by-step method of acquiring practical management skills*.

You're Hired....
You're Fired!

A Manager's Guide to
Employee Supervision

Deborah L. Whitworth

ISBN: 1-55270-146-8

Written by:
Deborah L. Whitworth

Published in Canada by:
Productive Publications, P.O. Box 7200,
Station A, Toronto, Ont. M5W 1X8
Phone: (416) 483-0634   Fax: (416) 322-7434

Front Cover Art:
Flames adapted from copyright free clip art from *Corel Gallery 200,000*
Corel Corporation, 1600 Carling Ave.
Ottawa, Ont. K1Z 8R7

Canadian Cataloguing in Publication Data

Whitworth, Deborah L.
    "You're hired....you're fired!": a manager's guide to employee
supervision / by Deborah L. Whitworth

ISBN 1-55270-146-8

    1. Supervision of employees. I Title

HF5549.12.W48 2004   658.3'02   C2004-902294-6

CONTENTS

33.00 LS July 04

Contents

EXECUTIVE SUMMARY

I've written *"You're Hired. . .You're Fired"—A Manager's Guide to Employee Supervision* for middle managers, department managers, human resources managers, supervisors, and those interested in working as managers or supervisors one day. Having practiced as a human resources manager for over 20 years, I've seen a lot. Management isn't hard to do but it is a process. I think those who I've worked with will tell you that I've served, most of the time, as a good role model. I make managing simple: I teach by example and I try to do the right thing. I educate myself, I allow myself to make mistakes, and I allow those whom I work with to make mistakes. I don't lecture. I teach by modeling behavior. Management is not an exact science. It is an art form. Some of us happen to be born with more talent than others. Not everyone is management material. Admit that, accept that, and move on to something you're more suited for.

I've written this book for you. You want to do the right thing. Unfortunately, nobody has told you yet what the right thing is. I'll tell you what the right thing is. I'll give you the step-by-step guidance you need to decide whether or not you're management material. You may not be. Or you may just need a little help. I'm the role model you need and I'm going to tell you, quite simply, how to manage yourself so you can be free to manage others. I'll share with you some memories from my past experiences working as a human resources manager in a variety of industries. Practicing good management doesn't come easy to all managers. Acquiring practical management skills that you can use in a step-by-step format is the goal of this book.

"You're Hired....You're Fired!"
A Manager's Guide to Employee Supervision

INTRODUCTION

You want to do the right thing. The trouble is that you don't always know what the right thing is. And the reason why you can't always identify the right thing is because nobody has ever told you what the right thing is. Probably what happened is that you were really good at doing _____. (You fill in the blank and we'll call it droxing.) In fact, many who you have worked with consider you an expert at droxing. When anyone in your department has a question about droxing, they probably come to you for an expert opinion. You were happy droxing. You enjoyed droxing. You were good at droxing.

Enter the Promotion Fairy. Isn't she pretty? The Promotion Fairy got her job because she was good at doing something. Just like you. . .she was happy crofting, she enjoyed crofting, and she was good at crofting. And she, like you, doesn't have a clue how to determine whether or not someone is ready for a promotion into management. But she was promoted into management because she was good at crofting. Not at managing. But something else entirely. Can you see where I'm going with this?

So one day, the Promotion Fairy taps you on the shoulder and says, "You're so good at droxing, that we've decided to make you a manager. Now you'll be managing people who are droxing." And you're flattered. This is a promotion. *The* promotion you've been waiting for. You've worked so hard at droxing and it's paid off. You'll make more money now. (You'll probably end up working more hours,

3

and now that you're a manager, you won't be eligible for overtime, so all in all, you're actually taking a pay CUT, but that's not the point.) You're flattered. You are a MANAGER. You're the Droxing Manager in your company. Wow! You have an official title. You get to order business cards. With your middle initial. Everyone will know you got a pay increase, even though it really was a pay cut, and anyway, now you are a MANAGER.

Let's think about this for a minute. Let's agree that managing is more than droxing and crofting. Can we agree that it's really accepting the responsibility to be responsible. And not just for droxing and crofting but for the people who will be droxing and crofting. And what do droxing and crofting and managing people have in common? Don't move on until you can answer this question. Think about this. What do droxing and crofting *and* managing the people who drox and croft have in common. I can see you're developing a brain cramp on this one. And this is an easy one! Okay, I'll tell you: NOTHING. Notice that NOTHING is in all caps? Take particular notice of this because if we were chatting over coffee right now, my voice would almost shrill and my pulse would increase as I said NOTHING.

Understand that managing people who perform a skill and performing that skill are not the same. Doing things that are not the same requires that you use different skills. And, unfortunately, the Promotion Fairy in your organization doesn't realize this. She thought that because you were great at droxing, you'd also be great at managing the people who drox. She thought these two things were the same. And because she thought that droxing and managing people who drox were the same, she also believed that you could jump from droxing to managing droxers in a single

4

leap. She was thinking hopscotch on the playground when what we're really talking about is the varsity high jump at one of the Class A high schools. She thought that as soon as she gets a manager for this department, she can cross that task off of her to-do list. She gets great satisfaction from crossing things off of her to-do list. Cross, cross, cross. And she thought she'd be a star because she just promoted someone who was great at droxing into a job that has nothing to do with droxing.

The Promotion Fairy lives in an imaginary land; let's call it "The Land of Pleth", where new managers follow in the footsteps of previous managers. They don't deviate, no matter what may happen, from the way things have been done by those who came before them. The Promotion Fairy doesn't realize that previous managers didn't know what they were doing either. She just knows that she promotes employees who are great at crofting, droxing, and prebbing because that's how it's always been done. And it's always worked. Hasn't it? Sure it has. Nod and smile here. Nod and smile!

Chapter 1

Fix the Job Description Using the Rule of Minimums

If you don't know what a job description is, you need more help than this book will be providing. Take a class, take two, maybe get a degree. But if you do know what a job description is, you may read on.

If you want to do the right thing, you'll have to learn how to do the thing right. This means that you'll have to start at the beginning--the beginning of the employment life cycle. The life cycle begins when you decide you have a position to fill. You get approval to fill that position. You want someone to start in that position in two weeks. Anyone to start in that position. In two weeks. Everything in a company happens in two weeks. Employees quit and give two week's notice. Employees get two weeks of vacation. If your plant shuts down, it will shut down for two weeks. You think in two- week `cycles. And you just need a body to do the job. Preferably NOW, but you'll settle for two weeks. You're not gonna do this job. You've DONE this job and now you don't have to do this job anymore. Two weeks. At the latest. Anyway, how long can it take to fill this job?

This job. What is this job anyway? Great place to start. Let's think about what this job is. What will the person who you eventually hire be doing? Hmmmm. Job description! Maybe you have one, maybe you don't. If you don't, shame on you. If you do, this next part won't be too difficult. This is where we'll start.

Whenever someone leaves a position, consider it an opportunity to rethink and even remake the job. How many times do you really get to start with a blank piece of paper? Well, you get to now. If you haven't looked at the job description for a while, the job probably has changed and you don't even know it.

Whether you do or don't have a job description for the position you'll be filling, let's discuss the process of writing a job description. If you have a job description, you'll have a starting point and may just need a red pen to make revisions. If you don't have a job description, get out a legal pad and a pen and start writing.

Why do you need a job description, anyway? If you don't know, you'll need to read this chapter TWICE. Let's start with the basics. What is the POSITION TITLE? If this is a new position, you may want to wait until the description is written before coming up with a title. If you are filling a position that has been vacated, you can start with the previous title, realizing that once the description is written, you may decide to change it to something that better fits the description.

What DEPARTMENT is this position in? Who will SUPERVISE this position? Probably to either you or to a supervisor. Don't fill in a name here, but the position title. What are the JOB TITLES SUPERVISED by this position? In the US, you need to be concerned with this position's FLSA STATUS (Fair Labor Standards Act). In other words, is this position exempt (does not qualify for) or non-exempt (does qualify for) from overtime? In Canada, unlike the US where the labor standards are federally regulated, legislation on hours of work and overtime varies to a significant extent across the country. In many jurisdictions, there is regulation of the permitted hours of work while in some others, there is little or no regulation. Be aware of your own jurisdiction's regulations.

Let's keep this as simple as we can. In the US, positions are non-exempt and qualify for overtime if, for the most part, the position is paid on an hourly basis. Once that position has completed 40 hours of work during the workweek, the position is paid overtime, no exceptions, at one and one-half times the hourly rate of pay. That's the law in the US. The same is generally true in Canada, however, employees are exempt from the overtime provision if they are employed in a supervisory or managerial capacity or in a capacity concerning matters of a confidential nature. In addition, salespersons who are paid in whole or in part by commission are exempt from the overtime provision as are those individuals who are in architectural, dental, medical, engineering, and legal professions. Domestic workers and farm and ranch workers are also exempt in Canada.

If you are an employer in the US and believe the position may be exempt from the overtime pay requirement and, consequently, not qualify for overtime, then the position must pass a series of "tests" developed by The US Department of Labor.

Bona fide executive and supervisory, administrative positions, and professional positions, are exempt from wage and hour overtime pay provisions, providing the position is paid on a salary basis (a payment guarantee) and performs exempt (executive, supervisory, administrative, or professional) duties. Additionally, outside sales positions don't have to be paid on a salary basis in order to be exempt from overtime pay requirements.

What does all of this mean? Simply, when you determine that a position will be paid a guaranteed salary, "not subject to reduction because of variations in quality or quantity of the work performed," the position is exempt. The position will be paid a salary, without regard to the number of hours worked. If you think about this, it makes sense. A managerial position will typically require more than 40 hours of work per week, and the person in that position will perform the job without regard to the actual number of hours worked. (Remember earlier, I talked about a "promotion" and how someone who was, prior to a promotion into management, filling an hourly position and how after the promotion that person may actually be taking a pay cut to fill the managerial position? This is why.)

In order to qualify for a *bona fide* exemption from overtime, the position must pass a test or two. First, if the position is executive or supervisory in nature, the position's primary duty must be the management of a department, a unit, or a division and the position must regularly (i.e., as its primary function) direct the work of two or more employees. Furthermore, the position must be authorized to either hire and fire or recommend to hire and fire other employees, the position must regularly exercise discretionary judgment, and the position must spend no more than 20 percent of work time performing non-exempt (not executive, supervisory, administrative or professional) work. In the case of retail or service positions, that increases to 40 percent.

Professional position exemptions exist when the position's primary duty is performing work which requires knowledge of an advanced type which typically requires additional education and/or training beyond high school, in addition to acting independently and exercising judgment. Artists, inventors, writers or those positions requiring talent are also exempt from overtime.

Administrative position exemptions must be paid a minimum salary of at least the current minimum wage to be exempt from the overtime pay requirement and the primary duties must be performing office or non-manual work directly related to the management of the company, department, division, or unit. Additionally, in order to qualify for an administrative position exemption, the position must exercise discretion and independent judgment.

Outside sales positions are easy. If this position is typically away from the place of business making sales or trying to make sales and the position spends less than 20 percent of the time performing non-exempt tasks, the position is exempt from the overtime pay requirements.

Again, if you are a Canadian employer, it is important that you become familiar with your own province's regulations as they vary greatly from jurisdiction to jurisdiction.

This is a lot to think about. It's also a very important part of developing a job description. The penalties and fines imposed on employers who do not pay overtime to employees in those positions that are non-exempt can be staggering. Don't take this lightly. Classify the position you are going to fill correctly and put the FLSA (Fair Labor Standards Act) status on the front of the job description.

Positions are not "salaried" positions simply because it's easier for payroll or because you don't want to pay overtime.

The next section of the job description is called GENERAL DESCRIPTION OF RESPONSIBILITIES. This is simply a paragraph that describes the basics of the position. If, for instance, you're writing the job description for an administrative assistant, this paragraph might read like this:

> The administrative assistant will provide general clerical and administrative support to the department manager by answering the phones, transferring calls, and taking messages, by producing documents using a word processing program, by producing spreadsheets, as well as maintaining files, following up with clients as assigned, and scheduling appointments. Additionally, as time and the schedule permit, this position will provide back up support to the front office staff, cover for vacations, and order office supplies, perform additional responsibilities as required and as assigned by the supervisor. (I like this sentence and put it or something like it in all of my job descriptions.) This section also is where you will give a description of the mental abilities needed for the job. For instance, if you need an individual who can make quick decisions, multi-task, is mentally alert, and is well organized, this is where you would outline those requirements.

After you determine what the position will be responsible for accomplishing, you need to consider what experience and background someone filling the position will need. In this case, we use the *Rule of Minimums*. The section is entitled, EXPERIENCE, and you must consider the minimum number of years of relevant experience you will accept for someone filling this position. This is important because in determining this minimum requirement to be filled, you are creating your benchmark for interviewing future job applicants. If you determine that three years is the minimum you will accept then an applicant with two years will not meet this minimum requirement and will not, therefore, be interviewed. Think very carefully about the minimum you will accept and what you believe is truly needed for someone to be successful in this position. It may also be important to consider an individual's command of the English language, if, in fact, that is relevant to the position. It may be necessary for an individual filling a customer service position to be able to read and write English fluently; however, it may be less of a necessity for someone filling a programmer position. Conversely, if clients of your company are from varied ethnic backgrounds, it may be necessary for you to consider only applicants who have command of other languages in addition to English.

The next section, EDUCATION, is also governed by the *Rule of Minimums*. If you are going to require a bachelors degree, for instance, then you will not be interviewing applicants who have an associates degree. If you are going to require a high school diploma, you will also want to consider candidates qualified if they have received a or General Equivalency Diploma (GED) in lieu of attending high school. In making these decisions, carefully consider what is truly required. Is the education the key to success in this position, or is it the relevant experience, as described above. Once you make this decision, it is your benchmark for determining who will be interviewed and who will not. A sentence I like to use is, "relevant experience, in lieu of education, will be considered."

You're about half way done with your job description. The next two sections are applicable to US employers only and have to do with the Americans with Disabilities Act and determining the essential functions of the job. I'll make this real easy. PHYSICAL DEMANDS (in a usual workday) is the next section. You'll be assessing the physical demands required to complete the essential job functions. Essential job functions are those functions that, without them, there would be no job. You'll be determining how many hours per shift the position stands, sits, and walks. And then you'll determine at one time, how many hours per shift does this position stand, sit, and walk. Again, essential functions only. Let's look at the administrative assistant again. If the person in that position must sit for two hours at a time, in a typical day, in order to complete the word processing, filing, and clerical tasks, then, because those are essential functions of the job, then that's what must be written in this section.

If the position requires an individual to walk from one department to another and then across the parking lot to deliver mail and then to the building next door to pick up mail, those are all essential functions of the job—without those functions, the job would not exist and therefore again they must be written in this section. If the walking from building to building is simply ancillary to this position, i.e., anyone could do that and, in fact, several individuals in the front office take turns to accomplish this task, then walking from building to building is not an essential function. Don't consider simply what the position *can* do, but what it *must* do, physically, in order to exist.

Also as a part of PHYSICAL DEMANDS, you must consider the approximate percentages of time certain physical tasks are performed in carrying out the essential functions of the position. In this section, you'll again be considering essential job functions, but more specifically in terms of physical tasks. Again, let's consider the administrative assistant. The person in this position spends 40 percent of the day at the computer, producing word processing documents and spreadsheets. This is an essential function of this job, because without the production of word processing documents and spreadsheets, the job would not exist. Perhaps this position requires an individual to replenish the paper supply for the copy machine. This task requires that the individual be able to lift a 50-pound box of paper. This task comprises a minimal amount of time and could easily be taken on by someone else in the organization, i.e., if there is someone else in the organization who could do it. In a small organization, however, this might, indeed, be an essential job function.

The last section is a paragraph that outlines GENERAL WORK ENVIRONMENT. If the work environment is an office, the paragraph might read:

> The office setting is quiet but busy with clients, employees, and visitors coming and going throughout the shift. Everyone entering the building must sign in and then sign out when exiting the

building. This professional office environment requires the individual in this position to dress modestly.

If this administrative assistant works in a car dealership, the paragraph may read very differently:

> The lobby area of the car dealership can be busy, with customers and employees coming and going throughout the shift. The noise level of the shop located behind the lobby can be heard when the shop door opens and closes. Because the lobby is adjacent to the shop, the sounds and smells of the shop are apparent at all times. The individual filling this position will dress casually, realizing that frequent trips to the shop are part of the job.

Once you have completed the job description for the position you intend to fill, you'll be ready for signatures. The person submitting the job description (usually the manager) signs first, noting title and date, then the person filling the position (this will be kept blank until the position is actually filled) and finally, if you have one, the HR executive or, in lieu of that, the operations manager. It might also make sense to have a space for at least the employee filling the position to print his/her name above the signature line.

And that's it! Let's see what a job description format format for a US employer actually looks like. Canadian employers can eliminate the sections explaining FLSA status and Physical Demands.

POSITION TITLE   Job Description

POSITION: *Title of Position*
DEPARTMENT: *Name of Department*
SUPERVISOR: *Title of Supervisor*
JOB TITLES SUPERVISED: *If appropriate, list positions supervised*
FLSA STATUS: *Exempt or Nonexempt*

GENERAL DESCRIPTION OF RESPONSIBILITIES

EXPERIENCE

EDUCATION

PHYSICAL DEMANDS (in a usual workday)

Sit	Total hours/day	0.0	Hours at one time	0.0
Stand	Total hours/day	0.0	Hours at one time	0.0
Walk	Total hours/day	0.0	Hours at one time	0.0

Approximate percentages of time tasks are performed in carrying out the *essential* functions of this position:

      0%   of time bending/stooping
      0%   of time squatting
      0%   of time crawling
      0%   of time climbing
      0%   of time reaching above shoulder level
      0%   of time kneeling
      0%   of time hand/fingers used for repetitive motion
      0%   of time feet used for repetitive movements
      0%   of time hands/fingers used for fine manipulation
      0%   of time hands/fingers used for simple grasping
      0%   of time hands/fingers used for pushing/pulling
      0%   of time hands/fingers used for firm grasping
      0%   of time head/neck in rotational movements
      0%   of time head/neck in static position
      0%   of time head/neck in extension movements
      0%   of time head/neck in flexing movements

      Pounds employee is required to carry   0 lbs.
      Usual distance carried   0 ft.
      Pounds employee is required to lift   0 lbs.

Submitted by_____Date_____

_____Date_____
              Employee Signature

_____
              Employee Print Name

Human Resources Manager_____Date_____

Once you've completed this exercise, you'll need to determine the pay for this position. Notice I said "pay for the position." Pay the position, not the person. Repeat this 10 times, fast. By determining rate of pay at this stage of the process, you will be more apt to pay the position instead of the person you want to hire. Again, if you're filling a position that has been vacated, you'll have a good idea of what the pay range is. If this is a new position, you'll have to do some research in order to determine a fair rate of pay.

Determining a fair rate of pay. How do we do that? If you have at your disposal regional salary surveys, this is a good place to start. You can also get regional salary ranges from various Web sites. One I like and have used is *www.salary.com*. The database is fairly extensive and, although you will not get an exact rate of pay you can assign to your position, you will get ranges that you can use. You can talk to other industry managers at companies like yours to determine actual rates of pay. Typically, if you share information with them, they'll share it with you. Call temporary agencies to see what the going rate is, look at recruitment ads in the newspaper; sometimes rates of pay are provided in the ad. Browse Internet job posting boards like *www.jobsinme.com*. That's the one I use all the time because it has the most "real" jobs in Maine and I've had great success using it.

Now you're ready to recruit for the position you have open. Many organizations have internal job posting practices, and I believe that this is a good idea. By posting positions internally you give current employees an opportunity to make lateral job changes or to apply for positions that may be promotion opportunities. I don't believe it's ever a good idea for a company to say that it will post EVERY job that it has open because this is unrealistic. There may be times when an executive is hired for an organization and because upper management wants that person on board, they'll create a position for him or her. That position will not be posted. It will be created. Companies that do post internally should do so by instituting the practice of recruiting internally and externally at the same time. As an organization, don't say that an internal candidate will always get the position if s/he is the best qualified (since you'll be hiring the *best fit* anyway, this is a moot point). That is unrealistic. You should practice hiring the *best fit* for the position that is open, whether it means accepting an internal candidate or hiring an external candidate. As a manager you should never feel forced (a union contract notwithstanding here) to hire someone you don't want to work with. Practice choice by hiring the candidate who *fits* the position best at the time the position is open.

Let's talk about internal candidates. When you've posted a position internally, you are inviting current employees to explore an opportunity. Whether or not an internal applicant meets even the minimum qualifications for the open position, I believe it is your responsibility as the hiring manager to at least interview the internal applicant. The interview may only be a short discussion about why s/he cannot be considered for the position. But you have extended a courtesy and invited the employee to talk with you. Maybe if s/he is very interested, you can offer some advice on how s/he could bcould become q a position is open
in the future, you could consider him/her. (Notice I didn't say HIRE him/her. I said CONSIDER. Never make the hiring promise because it is one you'll have to keep. Keep your options open.) If the internal applicant is qualified for the position, then you can schedule him/her along with the rest of your applicants and let him/her

know what your process is, making particular note that you'll be hiring the *best fit* for the open position and that you will be interviewing external applicants as well as internal applicants.

The level of the position that is open will help you to determine your geographical recruitment boundaries. An hourly production position probably dictates a local recruitment effort, while a higher level, management position may involve a regional or national search.

Certainly you can recruit by placing an ad in the newspaper. You may determine that a Sunday ad is preferable to a Wednesday ad. Or your big weekly paper may be a Saturday paper. If you are recruiting for a professional position, you may find it helpful to conduct a national search where you'll advertise in professional journals. Companies that have more than just a few positions open at one time find it useful to attend job fairs and/or recruit over radio and/or cable TV.

You may find it helpful to work with a recruitment firm. Many recruitment firms offer *temporary to regular* services where, for a reasonable fee, you can "try out" a candidate before making a hiring commitment. The recruitment firm handles advertising and screening. Typically you're presented with only several well-qualified individuals to choose from. Companies that do not have an HR function find this type of recruitment particularly cost effective. If you are recruiting for a supervisory or management position, you may find it beneficial to work with an executive recruitment firm that will charge a percentage of the first year's salary upon placement. Again, if you do not have an HR function, or if you are recruiting for a difficult-to-fill specialty, you may find it beneficial to work with a recruitment firm. There are various websites that are quite useful and often very cost effective. Determine your recruitment budget and spend your dollars wisely.

Regardless of your recruitment venue, you'll need to specify whether you'd like to receive resumes or have applicants come to your office to complete job applications. This will be included in all of your advertisements as well as contact information. I find it very snobby when companies do not include contact information, but simply ask applicants to respond to a department. Granted, busy managers may not find it a good use of their time to answer phone calls. However, we give a wonderful impression of ourselves when we include a name with contact information. The applicant who wishes to send a cover letter can then address it to a person rather than to a department. Perhaps the applicant has a question about the specifics of the job that s/he would like answered prior to applying. Time can be saved on his/her part and yours when you just answer the question. I don't believe I'd like to work for a company that includes in its ads a statement like "so we may review resumes promptly, we thank you in advance for not calling us." Typically, those are the companies that respond to applicants only when the job has been filled. They really don't care that applicants are waiting for a response. Their concern is simply one-sided. You've just spent a great deal of your company's money on your recruitment effort. Answer your phone, answer the question, and provide much needed customer service to your most important customers of the moment—potential employees!

Chapter 2

Don't Botch the Interview

Once you're in recruitment mode, you will begin receiving resumes and/or applications. Pull out the job description you've spent so much time writing and compare each resume to the minimums you've required in the job description. If your *Rule of Minimums* is two years of relevant experience, then an applicant with six months of experience is put in the "no" pile. If you have required a bachelor's degree, then you can't interview an applicant with an associate's degree. And so on until you have a pool of applicants in your "yes" stack that can be invited for interviews. At this point, you will determine how many applicants you'd like to invite for interviews. Because all of the applicants in your "yes" stack are qualified for the job (they meet the minimum requirements in both experience and education), you'll have to make decisions on how many applicants you'd like to actually interview. If you have 10 in your "yes" stack but really just want to interview three, you can screen all 10 with a 10 minute phone conversation and then make your decisions on who to invite in for a formal interview based on the results of the phone conversations.

Phone screening is handled much the same way an interview is handled except that it is done over the phone and it takes considerably less time. This time, however, is time well spent because you may determine during your 10 minute screening that the applicant really isn't interested because the job is too far away from where s/he lives. Or maybe the applicant is currently earning a higher salary than the upper range of the salary you're willing to pay and a pay cut is not an option for the applicant. You should have a list of five or so questions that you'd like to ask each applicant during the phone screening, along with a brief introduction of who you are and who the company is, so that you can make your decisions on who will be invited for an interview based on the results of the phone screening. The phone screen should go like this:

Once you have the applicant on the phone,

> *Hi, Sally, this is Peter from XYR Company. You've applied for the position of administrative assistant with our company and because of the number of well-qualified applications we've received, I'd like to take a few minutes and conduct a brief phone screening. If this isn't a good time, when could I call you?*

> *Sally, as you may know, XYR Company is a shoe manufacturer located in Pasco. Tell me a little about what you know of our company. (This is asked for a few reasons. First, has the individual done any research on your company? And, second, depending on what s/he knows, you may or may not provide company information.)*

> *Sally, the position you've applied for, administrative assistant, will be responsible for a variety of functions. Essentially, the individual who is hired will report to the Executive Vice President for*

Domestic Operations. Can you tell me, briefly, about your work experience and why you believe you'd be a good fit for this particular position.

This position requires that the individual who is hired is able to do a variety of tasks and switch from task to task throughout the workday. Can you give me an example, either in your current position, or in a past position, of how you've been able to successfully multi-task throughout your workday?

The individual we hire for this position will also cover the reception desk while that person is on break and at lunch. Can you give me an example of when you may have been responsible for similar coverage at another job you've held?

Sally, I'm interested in why this position is of interest to you. Can you tell me why you'd like to work with XYR Company?

It seems like you're happy at your current position (if this is true). I'm wondering why you're interested in leaving your current employer.

And, finally, Sally, could you share with me your salary expectations.

That's probably plenty of screening questions. You'll get a good sense of Sally's motivation for leaving her current employer, whether or not she's interested in the position as you've described it, and whether or not she sees herself as a good fit for this position. Additionally, you'll know whether or not her salary expectations are in line with those of your company. You'll be taking notes during the screening so that when you've completed all phone screens, you can prioritize your applications and decide who to bring in for face-to-face interviews.

A screening interview also works well if you're conducting a national or more wide-spread search and will save your organization time and money. You'll bring in only applicants who have been screened and meet the above criteria, are interested in making a move, and have salary expectations that your organization can meet.

You've conducted your screening interviews and are now ready to invite the top applicants in for formal face-to-fact interviews. If you have not conducted screening interviews, then this will be the first interview for your applicants, and possibly the only interview before you make a hiring decision. It's important, again, to have prepared questions for your interviews so that you ask each applicant the same questions, so that you take good notes, and so that you can make a well-informed decision at the end of the process. Since you'll only be interviewing applicants who meet the minimum job requirements, you'll be interviewing to determine which candidate will be the best fit for the job you have open. Notice I didn't say, the applicant who is the best qualified. "Best qualified" can always be debated and discrimination issues can surface. By instituting a practice of hiring the "best fit" for the job, you eliminate potential discrimination because "best fit" is a subjective judgment, rather than an objective decision which is based on criteria that can be measured. If you were hiring the best qualified, you would hire the applicant with the most years of experience and the highest degree received. In fact, you could hire most likely from the resume and not even interview! That applicant may not, however, be the best fit. Rather, the best fit will also meet the minimum requirements (remember the rule of interviewing only those applicants who do meet the minimum requirements), but may not have the MOST qualifications or the MOST years of experience. You believe, however, that s/he will be the best fit for the job, the department, and the company based on your experience working with and/or supervising the department members. As long as you practice "best fit" you can make subject judgments because you're only interviewing qualified applicants to begin with.

The interview process will go like this. Make your calls to invite applicants in for interviews. Introduce yourself, ask if this is a good time to talk for a minute, and then briefly describe the position (if a screening interview did not take place; if it did some of this may be omitted). Invite the applicant for an interview by giving him/her several choices of times and dates that may fit into his/her schedule. You may want to share with the applicant company information that may make him/her more comfortable. For instance, if your company practices "business casual" or "casual" either daily or on the day the candidate will be interviewing, s/he may be more comfortable during the interview if dressed appropriately. Showing up in a suit when everyone else is walking around in jeans can make the applicant uncomfortable. And that's the opposite of what you're trying to achieve. You want to give the applicant every opportunity to fit in so that when you're faced with making a hiring decision, you can make it based on fit.

I interviewed several years ago with a rather progressive company that practiced "casual attire" daily. At the time I was working for a rather "stuffy" organization that practiced the antithesis of casual. Suits, stockings, and high heels made up my daily ensemble. I was going to the interview on my lunch hour and was wearing a black skirt, medium high pumps, a white blouse, and a multi-colored blazer. I walked into the company and everyone was wearing jeans, tennis shoes, and sweatshirts. I immediately felt out of place and quite overdressed.

The first person to interview me was the individual, let's call her Bebee (for bleach blond) who I would be working with. In fact, I was interviewing for the position of her supervisor. During the interview, I noted that everyone was dressed casually, except her. So I asked if the company practiced casual attire daily. She confirmed that and said, rather proudly, that on days she conducted interviews, she dressed up to make a good impression and to give candidates the best impression of the company that she could. Translation: She was giving applicants a view of the company that was not realistic. (I made a mental note of this.) The interview was rather strained and I got the impression that she really didn't like me. Before it was over, a gentleman stuck his head in (I later learned he was one of the company co-founders) and introduced himself. He smiled widely and asked what I was doing there. His wide grin was contagious and I smiled in response and told him I was interviewing for the HR Director position. He then said, "Oh, Bebee, you're interviewing your future boss!" She blushed and he and I carried on a bit of small

28

talk. He told her that when she was done, he'd like to speak with me. He left and Bebee brought the interview to an abrupt end. She allowed me to follow her to his office where he'd been joined by the CFO, who was equally entertaining. We laughed as I answered questions and I felt as though I'd known both of them for years. It was obvious each of them had a great deal of interview experience. When one of them asked why I was all dressed up, and didn't I realize NOBODY dressed up there, and if I was offered the job, did I own any jeans. . .well, I smiled and said that I really wasn't made aware of the dress code.

I was offered the position the next day by the CFO. And I accepted it on the spot. This was the type of company I wanted to work for and both the co-founder and CFO were individuals I wanted to work with. Bebee, on the other hand, would be a challenge. During my orientation with the CFO, I was told that she had approached him several months before asking for an assistant, and he told her that what she actually needed was a boss. (That would be me.) He also told me I had carte blanche to make any changes I felt necessary.

On my second day, I met with Bebee and during our conversation I let her know that from now on when we were scheduling interviews, we'd be letting applicants know that the company was "casual" so they'd feel comfortable. I also said that we would be dressing casually, daily, even on days when we had interviews. Bebee was not happy with that change and asked, about two months later, for a change in duties. I was all too happy to comply. I changed her job function, and about a month later, moved her to a department more compatible with the new job: accounting. She was handling transactions, rather than dealing with people. This was a great fit for her in my judgment. It was ironic then that during one of our conversations prior to the change, Bebee noted that "All I really ever wanted to do was manage." Oh puleeeeze. A manager, never. But she was great controlling paper transactions. I then promoted someone internally to be my new assistant. She was a gem and a pleasure to work with. I was a great fit for the company, but unfortunately, I was not a great fit for Bebee.

The point of this story is to illustrate why fit is so important. Give your applicants a true picture of the organization. If your company is casual, don't wear a suit on the days you interview. Tell your applicants up front so they feel comfortable from the moment they walk in the door. If you happen to be conducting interviews on a "casual Friday" then dress casually and invite your applicant to do the same with the explanation that it's "casual Friday." Your applicants are interviewing you, on behalf of your company, as well, and they will be making a decision at the end of the process, too.

If you allow flexible scheduling in your department, explain how that works and to what extent it is allowed and offered. It could make a big difference with the applicant you finally offer the position to. Share company information and job-pertinent information will be shared with you.

Once you're ready to start the interview process, you'll need to script your interview to a certain extent. You may want to start with a brief history of the company, talk about what the company does, talk more specifically about your department, and then discuss why the position is open, whether it is a new position or replacing an employee who has left. You do not, however, need to detail why the individual has left a position if, in fact, you are replacing someone whose employment was terminated. You can be brief by stating that the position is open due to an employee's departure. Have your company history jotted down in bullet form and then develop your interview questions. You'll be asking behavioral interview questions. That is, questions that ask for relevant examples of what an applicant has done in the past. These types of questions elicit answers that will shape how s/he performs tasks, makes decisions, and produces work in the future.

Let your receptionist know that all applicants will be completing a job application and reference authorization forms. That means EVERY applicant for EVERY job your company has open will be completing a job application. There are a few reasons for this. By having applicants complete a job application, you are able to look at information presented in the same format for each applicant. Use an application that you've ordered from a forms company that includes a copyright date. That way, you know the information is in compliance with any changes in employment law. You may NOT simply order one pack of job applications and copy them for continued use, nor may you copy a copyrighted job application you've received from a friend. That is a violation of copyright law. Order the job applications and have each applicant complete one. Make sure you use applications that have a space noting starting and ending salary for each position the applicant has held. This will give you the applicant's salary history in a nutshell. Most applications also have a space for the applicant to list desired salary for the position applied for. Discussing salary can be difficult for managers and by having this information in front of you, you'll be able to lead into those questions more easily.

31

There is also a statement on the job application that inquires about prior convictions as well as a paragraph noting that all information contained on the application is true. The signature further confirms that the information contained is true.

By having written reference authorization forms prepared for each applicant to complete, you allow the applicant to choose who will be contacted for a reference. This does not mean that you shouldn't inquire about former supervisors listed on the job application who are NOT chosen as a reference. In fact, you most definitely should ask! This step in the process gives you three written references that you may then call to ask follow up questions of. As a diligent hiring manager, it is important to obtain written references for applicants who you consider as finalists for the position that is open.

By using job applications, you also have employment information in the applicant's own handwriting. Resumes can contain typos, perhaps even typos for years spent at a particular company. Where the resume shows an applicant worked for a company from June of 1980 to January 1991, the applicant was only there from June 1990 to January 1991. Oops. . .typo! Quite a different employment history picture. If you were using just the resume as the employment map, you may never think to question length of service. However, the job application would not contain a typo and you would then be in a position to inquire as to why the applicant was only at that particular company for just over six months. Resumes contain the information *the applicant* wants you to have. Job applications contain the information *you* need to have. Do not accept "see resume" as a substitute for information required on the job application. Give the applicant time to fill in the blanks. If someone can't take the time to fill in all of the blanks, you have to ask yourself how thorough this applicant will be in completing job responsibilities if hired.

Once the application is completed, you'll greet the applicant in the reception area and take him/her to where you'll be conducting the interview. If you don't have a private office or cubicle, reserve some space in your company that is private, so that you can give the applicant your full attention during the interview. Unless there is an emergency, you should not answer your phone, and you should ask your receptionist to hold your calls until your interview is completed.

After a brief introduction of the company, its history, and your position with the company, you'll move into the interview itself. Frame your job-related questions around those that follow, based on the position itself. It's important to keep your questions job related because that is what you will base your hiring decision on. By asking all applicants the same questions, you steer clear of asking certain questions to only applicants of certain ethnic backgrounds, for instance. That can be viewed as discrimination and that's definitely something you'll want to avoid. By asking the same prepared job-related questions to each candidate, you limit your exposure to a potentially discriminating situation.

Type your questions and leave space between them so you can take good notes. You will not be taking notes on the job application, which is a legal document when signed by the applicant, not on the resume. Only take notes on your question sheet. You'll be asking questions in a way that most applicants aren't familiar with.

You'll need to be patient and give each applicant the time s/he needs to think of specific examples. Don't feel as though you have to move on when an applicant can't come up with an answer. Simply pause and say that you have plenty of time for the applicant to think of an example.

To begin the interview you can say something like, "I'd like you to know that I've prepared a variety of questions and I'd like you to give me some specific examples as we move through the interview. I'll be taking notes, as I will with all the applicants I'm interviewing, so I can make a good hiring decision. Please feel free to take notes of your own and be assured that there will be plenty of time at the end for you to ask your own questions of me."

"You're applying for the position of administrative assistant. I'd like you to give me a brief history of your career, starting with your first job as clerk at the County office."

"Thank you. That was very informative. As you can imagine, the position of administrative assistant is a very busy one. And it sounds like you've had positions in the past that have been equally as busy, requiring that you do a variety of tasks, moving from one task to the next, throughout the day. I'd like you to give me an outline of what yesterday was like at your current job." (Notice, we don't ask for a "typical" day. There are no typical days. And you want to start the applicant off right by giving you specific examples, not vague generalities.)

"It sounds like you had your hands full yesterday. As I said over the phone, this position is also responsible for covering the reception function while that individual is on break and at lunch. Can you give me an example of another position you've had that has required you to cover for another individual on a regular basis?"

"Can you give me an example of a project you've completed that you're proud of?"

"The job you're applying for requires exceptional customer service skills. Our customers can be other employees, clients, vendors, or visitors. I'd like you to give me an example of a particularly difficult customer service dilemma you've encountered and walk me through the process you used to reach a conclusion."

"Can you share with me an experience you've had that will give me a good indication of your multi-tasking skills?"

"If you've ever had to work with difficult people, you'll know that we're not always able to choose our coworkers and that sometimes personality conflicts can wreak havoc in the workplace. Can you give me an example of a particularly difficult person you've had to work with and how you've managed to work with him or her?"

"Time management is important in this job, as I'm sure it is important with your current position. Can you outline for me your methods for effective time management, starting with how you start your day and ending with how you complete your day?"

"Can you describe for me the traits of an individual you've worked with who you admire and respect and explain why?"

"Can you give me an example of a difficult situation you've encountered at the workplace and explain how you were able to work through it?"

"Can you give me an example of a time you were considered an expert at something and explain to me how you handled the requests of others who asked for your advice?"

"What is the job that you've liked the most and give me examples of why you liked it."

"And tell me about the job you've liked the least and why you didn't like it."

"Tell me about how you have learned how to do something that you were asked to do but didn't know how to do it."

"We all make mistakes, and I'm sure you're no different. Could you give me an example of a mistake you've made on the job and explain what you did?"

"Can you tell me about a time you made a quick decision that was also a very good decision?"

"Can you tell me about a time that you were forced to make a quick decision that was not a good decision?"

"Can you give me an example of a project that you've worked on when the results were something you were not proud of?"

"Of course I would not contact your current supervisor because you've noted that I may not. I understand that contacting her could put your job in jeopardy. But take a moment and explain to me how she would describe your work habits and your working relationship with her."

"I notice that you have not completed a reference authorization form for your supervisor at Company X. If I were to call this supervisor at your previous place of employment for a reference, tell me what he would say about you."

"You've listed three references on your application and you've also completed reference authorization forms for each of them. Please outline for me what each one of them will say when I follow up receipt of the reference form with a phone call."

"I've asked you a lot of questions, and I'd like to give you an opportunity to ask questions of me. But first, I'd like to outline our benefits program and give you some other information I think you'll find interesting." Then do this.

At this time, you invite the applicant to ask questions of you about the job, the department, and the company. Answer them honestly. Don't give the applicant answers you think s/he wants to hear. Be honest, without breaching company confidentiality or sharing proprietary information, and let him/her know what the future holds for the department and for the company. Don't paint a picture that you believe the applicant wants to see. Paint a realistic picture so that when you do make a hiring decision and that individual does accept the job, s/he is accepting a realistic job in a real company without surprises.

Interviewing in this way is probably different from the interviewing you're probably used to. This works. Instead of asking an applicant to paint a picture of how s/he would handle a particular situation, you're asking the applicant to tell you how s/he has handled a similar situation in the past. Past behavior is a good indicator of future behavior. Remember this. When we ask someone how s/he would handle a situation, we get a make-believe story that takes place in a picture-perfect world. But we want real-world answers. And to get those, we have to ask questions that give us examples of real ways that things have been handled in the past. It might not always be pretty. But it is real.

Consider these two questions. And answer them as though you were being interviewed.

"Providing exceptional customer service is one of the most important aspects of the job you're applying for. You'll be faced with tough situations from time to time. Tell me how you will handle difficult customers."

Now consider,

"Providing exceptional customer service is one of the most important aspects of the job you're applying for. Can you give me an example of a particularly difficult customer you've encountered in the past and explain to me, step by step, how you handled the situation you were faced with."

See the difference? Asking questions that require specific examples will give you information you can actually use because you'll get a realistic picture of the applicant you're interviewing.

Once you have answered the questions the applicant has asked, you'll need to outline your process: When will interviews be completed? When will the decisions be made? When will the applicant hear from you one way or another? Let the applicant know that if, after s/he gets home and has an additional question or two, s/he can contact you by phone or email and you'll be glad to provide answers. Give applicants a business card. Let the applicants know that the reference authorization forms will be sent out in today's mail and that until they are received, no hiring decision will be made. This gives the applicant the impetus to call those who s/he listed on the reference forms and urge them to complete the forms promptly. Otherwise, the form could sit on someone's desk for weeks before being completed.

Chapter 3

Don't Negotiate—Just Hire

Making a hiring decision is one of the most important decisions you'll ever make as a manager. Making a bad hiring decision can cost your company time, money, and end with a potential lawsuit. Making a good hiring decision by taking your time and giving the interview process the time and effort it deserves will help to ensure that you hire the best fit for the position you have open.

Determine who your final candidates are. Maybe you have one candidate who stood out from the rest and you've already decided that this is the person you'd like to offer the position to. Or you may have several candidates who you believe would all be a good fit for the position you have open. Gather all of your information: job applications, resumes, reference forms, and interview notes. Prioritizing candidates is a rather subjective process, so read all the information carefully, jot down additional notes if you need to, and make a decision based on who you believe will be the best fit with the people who are currently in your department, the culture of your company, and who will work cooperatively with you, as the manager. If you can't decide between two candidates, perhaps invite both back in for a final interview before making your decision.

Sometimes, listing the attributes of final candidates is a helpful process to work through in making the hiring decision. If you have two candidates that you cannot decide between, list the assets and liabilities of each on a sheet of paper. Be as objective as you possibly can. Usually after completing this process, one candidate or the other usually stands out as the best fit.

You have already developed a salary range when you wrote the job description. Now you'll have to determine the exact pay to be offered. You'll do this by looking at a few criteria. First, internal equity. What are others in the company with like experience and education earning who are doing a job that requires similar skills? If you don't have an exact position elsewhere in the department, look for one that is similar and pay comparably. It's important to determine exact rate of pay prior to making the job offer because job offers should NEVER be negotiated. That's right. Never. You may need to repeat this several times because you probably don't really believe it. If you have done your homework and you believe your job offer is fair (no, don't just pay the minimum you think you can get away with; pay fairly), there really is no room for negotiation. Is there? Where?

Whether you make the job offer in person or over the phone should be a decision you make with the candidate. A phone call could go like this:

Hi, Carla, this is Sue from XYR Company. I'd like to offer you the position of administrative assistant and I'd like to know whether you'd like to do that over the phone or if you'd prefer to come into the office. Many candidates will be so excited, they won't be able to wait to come in person. Other candidates may prefer doing it face to face. It's really a matter of personal preference and I like to give candidates the choice.

The conversation, whether in person or over the phone could go like this:

Carla, I'd like to offer you the position of administrative assistant. As we discussed, the position is responsible for (briefly outline duties) and will report to me (or someone else perhaps). After reviewing the salaries of similar positions, both within the company and in the area, I'd like to offer you a salary of $$$. As we also discussed, the position is eligible for a full benefits package, which employees contribute on a payroll deduction basis. You are also eligible for X weeks of vacation, which accrue as of the first day of employment. I'm hoping, if you accept, that you'll be able to start in two weeks.

If the candidate wants to negotiate salary, simply be firm and say, I don't negotiate salary because I've done a considerable amount of research even before I began the recruitment process. I need to be sensitive to my current employees and I'm aware that similar positions within the immediate area have a pay range of $$$ to $$$ and, based on your relevant education and experience, I believe a salary of $$$ is fair. You would be eligible for a pay increase in June. Last year our average pay increase was three percent, although that number is not set in stone. Let's talk about the benefits so you can get a true understanding of what total compensation is at XYR Company. Then outline the benefits package, what s/he will be contributing out of his/her pay, and have a discussion about time off, scheduling, and anything else that could make a difference. If the candidate is more interested in $$$ than the job, perhaps you've made a bad hiring decision. It would be appropriate, at this time, to let the candidate know that there really is no room for negotiating and perhaps this isn't a good fit after all. S/he may agree and decline the offer. Or s/he may say that it really isn't that big of a deal and s/he would like to continue with the conversation.

When you have the mindset that you'll negotiate pay, you are immediately on the defensive. Don't put yourself on the defensive. Once you start negotiating with a future employee, you'll spend a fair amount of time negotiating with that person as a current employee. The way the job offer is presented sets the tone for this individual's future with you and with the organization. You can be weak or you can manage. If you decide you want to be weak, you can stop reading this book. If you decide you want to manage, then start before the candidate begins working with you. Most candidates truly believe that there is always room for negotiation. Let your candidates know up front that there isn't. Your first offer is your best and only offer.

If the candidate accepts, agree on a start date. The candidate may ask to have a day or two to consider the offer. That's reasonable. Just agree on a date that you need the decision to be made. Once s/he has accepted the position, you'll need to agree to a start date. Be sensitive to the position the new employee is in and allow him/her to give as much notice as s/he considers appropriate. I've found, however, that notices beyond two weeks simply produce a lame duck. But if the current employer asks for more time, be as reasonable as possible because the candidate is in a difficult position. Once the start date is agreed upon, let the candidate know that a confirmation of offer letter will go out by the end of the day tomorrow.

The confirmation of offer letter is just that. It's not a contract but a letter that confirms the offer you made. There are a variety of opinions regarding how to state the rate of pay. Some HR professionals believe that if an annual salary is stated and, employment is terminated by the company during the first year of employment, then the entire first year's annual salary will be due the employee. There is no specific case law but some HR professionals, myself included, believe that if a rate of pay is quoted in an offer of employment letter, then the company could be held liable for fulfilling that "promise to pay" if the person and the position do not work out. If the position is exempt from overtime, you may feel more comfortable stating the monthly salary or even the weekly salary to avoid this possible issue and be "on the hook" for just a month or week of pay. You could then include the annual salary in parentheses. If the position is nonexempt, then you'll state the hourly rate of pay. The letter should read something like this:

Date

Inside Address

Dear NAME:

This letter confirms our offer of a full-time position as TITLE with COMPANY at a monthly salary of $3,000 ($36,000 annualized) beginning on DATE at TIME. This offer of employment is contingent upon verification of previous employment. As a full-time employee you may participate in our benefits program as a full-time participant effective DATE. Detailed information regarding our

benefits program will be available to you on your first day of employment.

[*For US Employers only*] Enclosed for your review is information regarding the Immigration Reform and Control Act of 1986. Upon accepting a position with COMPANY, the I-9 Form must be completed to verify identity and employment eligibility as required by law. You will be asked to complete an I-9 on your first day of employment with COMPANY. Please bring the appropriate documentation with you at that time.

No provision herein is to be construed as a guaranty of continued employment and all employees of COMPANY are employed at will. Any contrary agreement must be in writing and must be signed by the President of COMPANY. Moreover, this letter does not create any such contrary agreement or contract of employment.

We are looking forward to having you join our team and believe you will find the experience a rewarding one. Welcome to COMPANY!

Sincerely,

NAME
TITLE

Enclosures

Now that you have a new employee, it's appropriate to let those who were not hired know of your decision. A simple thank you letter can be sent to everyone who was not hired. It should not say anything about the individual having wonderful qualifications (if that's so, why wasn't s/he hired, anyway!). It can go like this:

Date

Inside Address

Dear NAME:

Thank you for applying for a position with COMPANY. Although we have filled this position, we will keep your application on file and active for six months. Should we have additional openings during that time, we may contact you.

Thank you again for your interest in COMPANY and good luck in your employment endeavors.
Sincerely,

NAME
TITLE

Chapter 4

Making Your New Employee Comfortable

I should have known that, when, on my first day of employment with the financial services company, that I had no place to sit as the new HR Director, I'd made a big mistake in accepting the position. I rationalized by saying to myself that once I was on board, things would be different for future new employees. Hah! Although I was given permission to make any and all necessary changes in order to make this employer one of Choice, that permission was snapped back after about nine months. The owner really liked things done his way and viewed my position as one of maintaining the status quo. WRONG! I left before I'd been there a year. Not a good fit.

Before the first day, determine where your new employee will sit. If this employee is filling a position vacated by an employee who has left the company, it may be very easy to determine where s/he will be sitting. If this is a new position, you'll have to decide where the new employee will be stationed. Once this is decided, you can prepare the workstation. The best way to welcome a new employee to the organization is to have his/her workstation prepared and somewhat ready to go. Of course, the new employee will want to personalize his/her workstation (to the extent that this is practical and your company allows this), but you can certainly have basic supplies stocked in the workstation. One company I worked with had "gift boxes" prepared for all new employees, based on the position that person was filling. The gift boxes were filled with standard supplies and the box (a copy paper box) was gift wrapped and left at the new employee's workstation. We then recycled the gift box itself as other new employees came on board. Typically, once a new employee is settled, s/he will require additional supplies. Based on your company's purchasing policies, you can acquaint him/her with purchasing guidelines and let him/her know how to place an order for whatever else is needed.

You're ready to greet your new employee. Do it personally when s/he arrives the first day. Ask the receptionist to let you know when the new employee arrives and meet him/her in the lobby. Shake his/her hand and welcome to the organization. Walk to where s/he will be sitting and let him/her deposit personal belongings. Then take a tour of the company. Show your new employee around the areas you believe are important, including where the restrooms are, the break room the smoking area (if there is one, either inside our outside), the first aid kit, the emergency exits, eye wash station, employee parking area, and where the Material Safety Data Sheet binder (MSDS) is kept. If you don't know anything about what a MSDS binder is, then you could be placing your organization at risk by not providing this information to your employees. In most organizations, the individual responsible for safety is responsible for compiling the MSDS binder and making it available to all employees. Each Material Safety Data Sheet provides valuable information on the substance or chemical that it is describing. This information includes what to do if an employee comes in contact with the particular substance or chemical and is provided upon request by the company that manufactures the chemical or substance. Another way to access the information is by going online to www.msds.com. You can print out individual Material Safety Data Sheets, put them in a binder, and have the binder accessible to all employees in a central location.

Then take the employee to every department and introduce him or her to the manager and any other key employees s/he may be interacting with in his/her new job. Introduce the individual to employees in your department and then allow the new employee to get settled in.

This first day on the job should be a day of orientation. Let your new employee read any company information you have. This will fill in the empty slots of the day and make you less responsible for entertaining your new employee. You'll also give your new employee a sense of ownership of his/her new job. S/he will start to be in control and begin on the right track to managing his/her time.

Don't leave him/her alone too long. The first day is really also the day of introductions—to people, to places, to process, and to functions. By leaving your new employee alone for a short time, you let him/her know that this is the time to get acquainted with the phone, the computer, and review the employee handbook. Review your company's break policy and, if applicable, let your new employee know when his/her break time is and where it may be taken.

By now it's time for lunch. It's your responsibility as the manager to have lunch with your new employee. You should provide lunch (even ordering sandwiches to eat in the break room) or take your new employee out for lunch. If that's not practical, make sure a coworker can fulfill this responsibility. Don't just leave your

51

new employee on his/her own! That can be a very intimidating experience and may not start the employment relationship on the right track. During lunch you might mention what many employees do for lunch. If yours is an organization where sandwich shops and/or restaurants are nearby, employees may make it a habit of stepping out for lunch. Perhaps many of your employees bring their lunch and eat in the break room. Maybe employees bring their lunch Monday through Thursday and order in on Fridays. Let your employee know that as well. Let your new employee know what the practice is in your department and in the organization.

After lunch, you'll have time to review the organizational chart and answer any questions the new employee may have. This is also a good opportunity to have the new employee sit with either a representative from human resources or payroll to complete necessary paperwork, benefits enrollment forms, and emergency contact information. Once the paperwork is completed, make sure you provide a list of employees and their extensions the new employee can contact for answers to questions regarding the phone, computer equipment and programs. Leave your new employee on his/her own with the invitation to call you at your extension if anything is needed. Check in at the end of the day to discuss the actual workstation and whether or not your new employee requires any ergonomic equipment. Discuss company guidelines for what is allowable under usual circumstances. If your new employee requires additional ergonomic supplies or equipment, you'll want to do what makes sense for your new employee, keeping in mind company guidelines and perhaps budgetary constraints. If your new employee seems to have many desires, you'll have to have a conversation about needs versus wants. It may also make sense to discuss requirements in terms of job function. A position that spends a great deal of time on the phone probably requires a headset. A position that spends a most of the day producing documents on the computer may need a combination mouse pad/wrist rest. Setting up purchasing guidelines for ergonomic equipment around job function also alleviates the "I want" syndrome surrounding current employees who also want the newest gadget but whose job function doesn't dictate that this newest gadget is a necessity.

Answer any questions that come up, outline what the second day will be like and then the rest of the week. If appropriate, you have arranged for your new employee to job shadow one or more employees and that can start on the second day. If that is not appropriate to the position, simply confirm that day one went well and talk about day two. Ask your new employee to check in with you at the beginning of day two so you can discuss work assignments for the day.

Your new employee should be settling in nicely and ready to either job shadow or to actually do some work on day two. At some point during day two, you'll meet your new employee to discuss how s/he would like to be supervised and what your thoughts are about supervision. This might not be a question s/he has ever been asked before so you might approach it this way: "I'd like to talk tomorrow about how you think you'd like me to provide supervision and direction. Think about what has worked well in past jobs and about what hasn't worked, in your opinion. We need to develop a plan that will work for both of us."

Chapter 5

Just Do It!

As a manager, it's important that you take day-to-day supervision of your employees seriously. The ability to provide your employees with solid supervision is what makes you a manager. The guidance, training, and support you provide enable your employees to do their jobs effectively.

The key to providing solid supervision is in finding a balance between what your employees need and what you can give. The people who report directly to you are entitled to meet with you on a regular basis. Defining whether "regular" means daily, weekly, bi-weekly, monthly, or quarterly is something you should do together with each one of your employees. Certainly a new employee, or one who is new to a particular job function, will require more of your time on a more regular basis than an employee who has been performing a job for several years.

Once this regular supervision session is scheduled, take it as seriously as you would any other meeting. You will be giving your employees your undivided attention during this meeting so try to make sure you aren't bothered with interruptions. My rule has always been, "if my kid isn't bleeding on the playground, I don't want to be interrupted." If you know you'll have to take a call that you've been waiting for, tell your employee at the beginning of the session that you may be interrupted, and why, and that you may have to excuse yourself for a few minutes.

Something I've done for years is to keep an ongoing file folder on every person under my direct supervision. In this folder, I put notes that I accumulate between supervision sessions. I keep a running agenda of things we need to discuss. By the time we meet, and I meet with different employees at different intervals based on our collective needs, I have my agenda prepared. If you use a calendar, planner, or electronic data device, you can keep a running agenda on a page or section devoted to each employee you supervise. When you do this, you do not add work should you find yourself in a position to provide discipline to this employee. And, further down the road, if you're faced with a discrimination claim or lawsuit, your notes are ready. Documentation is done as a part of your job, not in addition to it.

To make the meetings more meaningful, I also have each employee I supervise keep a file folder with my name on the tab. They also keep a running agenda of things we need to discuss from their perspective. By the time we meet, both of us have agendas prepared and the meeting moves along smoothly and we've spent our time well. An added bonus is that when employees have questions prepared for the meeting, they'll jot down the answers during the meeting. Now in addition to a productive meeting, they also have a ready reference for when that question comes up (and it will) again. It's less likely that, as your employees run to you with questions throughout the day, they will stop to jot down a note. Alas, no ready reference. Just constant interruptions.

Certainly, if something urgent comes up between supervision sessions, you'll need to be flexible enough to meet at that time. (You'll have to help your employees define "urgent.") But if your employee comes to you between supervision sessions with an issue that could clearly wait until the next session, tell your employee to put a note in your file and you'll discuss it then. If you take the time to address this non-urgent issue right then, you won't be modifying behavior and that behavior will continue. I promise.

Imagine for a moment, employees doing their jobs and not running to you every hour with the crisis of the moment. You and I know that all of these situations are not crises. But they are things that need to be addressed. If an issue affects your employee's work, then it should be addressed. The question relates to timing, "Does it have to be addressed NOW?" The answer is, "Usually not." By helping your employees to modify their behavior, you're helping them to become more productive employees.

Let's consider this scenario:

Employee to manager, "Mr. Smith is calling again with a question regarding how we plan to correct the mistake we made--again. I told him I'll call him right back. What should I tell him?"

Manager to employee, "I remember that you and I talked about a similar situation in a supervision session about two or three months ago. And I remember that you wrote down the answer because you and I knew it would come up again. Go check your notes and tell me what we decided and then you can call him back."

This is much better than a manager saying, "This comes up every few months. Can you remember how we handled it last time?" Or worse yet, "This comes up every few months. I'll take care of it once and for all." In the first two scenarios the manager can't quite remember what the agreed upon decision was. By going with the first scenario, you put your employee in the driver's seat by empowering him/her to resolve the situation AND you manage the situation. The second scenario illustrates what probably happens now. Neither you nor your employee has the answer and, unfortunately, you can't remember what has worked in the past. Rather than simply pulling out the first aid kit and getting yet another band-aid, like in the third situation, start acting out the first scenario. It works.

You can also use your regular supervision session to brainstorm ideas your employee has for doing a part of his/her job differently and, possibly, more efficiently. These sessions will also give you and your employee an opportunity to get to know one another better. Even though the purpose of the supervision session is to deal with work-related issues, you'll probably start most meetings with an ice breaker, a question about how his/her family is, or an inquiry about plans for the following weekend.

You'll find that once you've incorporated these supervision sessions into your department workflow, everyone will be more productive, including you. You'll find that, over time, employees will stop hovering around your office door or cubicle or workspace when the question is clearly one that can wait. You'll also find that those employees who keep a low profile, just do their jobs but go unnoticed, will become even more productive because they'll have your undivided attention during these supervision sessions. An idea that a shy employee may think is not worthy of your time could be a great idea! Without the supervision session, it will forever go unnoticed.

Even when you do everything right, you'll still be faced with an employee who isn't doing his/her job. You can provide your employees with everything they need to be productive. You can give them the tools they need, you can give them a pleasant work environment. You can provide them with attractive benefits. And you'll still have employees who can't or won't do the job.

Those two words, *can't* and *won't* are important to differentiate. Because whether an employee can't or won't do the job determines how you will handle the situation.

If you don't have a human resources department, your company may not have a disciplinary policy. And you'll need one so that you can address employees who won't do the job. By having a policy that your employees are aware of, they won't be surprised if you follow the guidelines outlined when someone won't perform the job.

If you do have a human resources department, you should have a policy in place that outlines your company's guidelines. If you don't, shame on your human resources manager. If you don't have a disciplinary policy, you can use the one that follows as a template to build one for your company.

If you are a Canadian employer, it's important to note that Canada has a Labour Standard that addresses the topic of Progressive Discipline. You can access this Standard at www.hrdc-drhc.gc.ca and typing in Progressive Discipline in the keyword search. The information provided is quite specific and easy to follow.

COMPANY NAME   **Policy and Procedure NUMBER**

DISCIPLINARY PROCEDURES

Date Effective: **DATE**

Authorized by: _____
                                                    President

POLICY

COMPANY reserves the right to discipline employees for violations of established COMPANY policies, standards of work, or actions that are dishonest, immoral, unsafe, illegal, or lacking in good judgment.

Disciplinary action can consist of a verbal or written warning, suspension, or dismissal depending on the seriousness of the offense. It is the policy of COMPANY to use a system of progressive discipline; however, an employee may be suspended or dismissed immediately for any action that suggests that continued employment threatens another employee, the clients we serve, or would create an unfavorable working environment for other employees.

PROCEDURE

The following steps will be followed in the processing of any disciplinary action:

1. The supervisor/manager will identify and investigate the incident or job performance behavior and gather pertinent facts.
2. The supervisor/manager will discuss the incident or job performance behavior with the employee.
3. The supervisor/manager will then issue a verbal warning, one or more written warnings, or one or a series of more stringent actions, depending on the severity of the violation. These actions may include probation, suspension, demotion, reassignment, or dismissal.

All disciplinary actions must be coordinated with the vice president of human resources (IF YOU DON'T HAVE A HUMAN RESOURCES DEPARTMENT, INSERT THE APPROPRIATE TITLE HERE) and appropriately recorded in the employee's personnel file.

RESPONSIBILITY

The administration of this policy is the responsibility of the management team.

FILING INSTRUCTIONS

This policy supersedes all previous policies on this subject. This policy will be filed in Section NUMBER of the COMPANY Policies and Procedures Manual.

An employee who won't do his/her job, is violating a company policy or practice and needs to be disciplined. But you need to be sure first that it is a situation of *won't*, not *can't*. You make this determination by observing the employee while s/he is at work, by listening to comments made by other employees (be sure to distinguish between a legitimate complaint and comments made about an employee who may be unpopular—you can do this by observing for yourself and by looking for patterns where numerous employees are making similar comments), and by reviewing your supervision notes on a regular basis. Other employees will not want to be carrying the weight of an employee who won't do his/her job. It's not fair to your other employees to be forced to pick up the slack. Take their comments seriously and observe fairly for yourself.

This employee who won't do his/her job is violating a company policy (if you have them) or a company practice (a full day's work for a full day's pay doesn't seem to be too much to ask of anyone). When this employee was hired, s/he said s/he could meet the schedule requirements, for example. And now s/he is not meeting the schedule requirements—s/he's coming in late once or twice a week. The job performance behavior that must be met dictates that employees report to work on time. S/he said s/he could when s/he was hired. And now, s/he's coming in late.

There could even be a good reason. But your concern isn't really with the reason, you're concerned with the outcome—which is that s/he is late and it's having an impact on the department and other employees.

Now, let's be fair. There could be a good reason why s/he is late all of a sudden. Before you jump into a disciplinary procedure, ask why s/he's all of a sudden is coming in late and requiring other employees in the department to pick up the slack. Maybe the employee is between child care providers, maybe s/he is having car trouble and hasn't had a chance to get a new car yet so has to rely on a neighbor, maybe his/her alarm clock broke last week and s/he hasn't had a chance to replace it. Maybe, maybe, maybe. There could be hundreds of very good excuses. However, the impact on the department and other employees is the same—they are picking up the slack.

You could ask this employee how much time s/he needs to have the situation corrected. Assuming that the time frame is not unreasonable, you could agree that no disciplinary action will take place until after that time. (If it is unreasonable, just say so and give an alternative that is reasonable.) You could also, depending on whether or not it makes sense, allow the employee to make up the time at the end of the shift until the situation is taken care of (again, in the time frame allotted). Be as reasonable as you can, keeping in mind the impact the behavior has on other employees. If the behavior continues after the time frame, you could then go through the disciplinary procedures.

Look at job performance behaviors only. Don't discipline an employee because s/he is having trouble getting up on time. Discipline for the job performance behavior—not meeting the schedule requirements (that s/he said s/he could meet during the interview process. . .remember?). Don't discipline because your employee can't seem to get the family out the door in the morning. Discipline for the job performance behavior—arriving to work late. Be reasonable and give your employee an opportunity to correct the behavior. Make sure your employee understands that arriving to work on time and consistently meeting the schedule requirements are job requirements. Do this the first time s/he is late. The second time, you can refresh your employee's memory, "Certainly you remember the conversation we had two weeks ago about the importance of meeting your schedule requirements and arriving to work on time every day. Did you understand when we met that arriving to work late is not acceptable?" Your employee will answer you, probably with a good reason. Good reason or not, the impact of this employee arriving late is felt in your department. And your comment will be something like, "As I explained several weeks ago, arriving to work late is unacceptable. Consider this conversation a verbal warning." Write up the conversation in memo form like outlined below:

MEMO
VERBAL WARNING

TO: **Employee Name**

FROM: **Your Name and Title**

DATE: **Date**

SUBJECT: **Not meeting schedule requirements**

We met several weeks ago, on DATE, and I discussed the importance of you arriving to work on time every day. You agreed that you could do that and, by doing so, you would be able to meet the schedule requirements we discussed during your interview.

You arrived to work late again this morning, thus not meeting your schedule requirements. Your inability to meet the schedule requirements you agreed to is due to your car being in the repair shop and you are forced to ride with a friend. Your car will be fixed by this Friday, DATE, and you have agreed that after that date you will be meeting your schedule requirements consistently.

Should you not meet your schedule requirements, further disciplinary action will follow, up to and including termination of employment.

Employee Comments

_____

_____

_____

_____

_____

_____

_____

_____

Employee Signature_____**Date**_____

Cc: Personnel File

We've done a few important things in this memo. Even verbal warnings should be documented. When an employee has a good reason for being late, for instance, it's important to give him/her an opportunity to correct the behavior. In this instance, s/he has a good excuse and there is a time when the behavior will no longer occur. This is acceptable but should still be documented. After the date (which you consider reasonable) you can expect the behavior to stop. If it doesn't, a written warning will follow and then possible employment termination. If the employee can't meet the schedule requirements, and if this is important in your department, then the job and the employee are not good fits for one another. You should find an employee who can meet the schedule requirements and this employee should find a job that isn't so strict where promptness is concerned.

Let's say that several months have passed and this employee, who agreed to meet the schedule requirements when you gave the verbal warning, is late one morning. After questioning him/her, you discover that s/he has car trouble again. Regardless of the reason for his/her tardiness, it's affecting the work in your department and it can't go on. So, you present the employee with a written warning.

MEMO
WRITTEN WARNING

TO: **Employee Name**

FROM: **Your Name and Title**

DATE: **Date**

SUBJECT: Not meeting schedule requirements

We met several weeks ago, on DATE, and I gave you a verbal warning because you were not meeting the schedule requirements. You said that you would be able to meet the schedule requirements by DATE and that, by doing so, you would be able to meet the schedule requirements we discussed during your interview.

You arrived to work late again this morning, thus not meeting your schedule requirements. Your inability to meet the schedule requirements you agreed to is having an adverse affect on the work flow in the department as well as employee morale. This cannot continue.

Should you not meet your schedule requirements after this date, your employment will be terminated immediately.

Employee Comments

_____

_____

_____

_____

_____

_____

_____

Employee Signature_____**Date**_____

Cc: Personnel File

The process is easy to follow. But this employee is late yet again and you are forced to terminate employment. The memo should look like this:

MEMO
EMPLOYMENT TERMINATION

TO: **Employee Name**

FROM: **Your Name and Title**

DATE: **Date**

SUBJECT: **Not meeting schedule requirements**

We have met several times, on **DATE, DATE, and DATE. On DATE, I gave you a verbal warning because you were not meeting the schedule requirements and on DATE I gave you a written warning because you were not meeting the schedule requirements. You said that you would be able to meet the schedule requirements by DATE and that, by doing so, you would be able to meet the schedule requirements we discussed during your interview.**

You arrived to work late again this morning, thus not meeting your schedule requirements. Your inability to meet the schedule requirements you agreed to is having an adverse affect on the work flow in the department as well as employee morale.

Effective immediately, your employment with COMPANY is terminated.

Employee Comments

_____

_____

_____

_____

_____

_____

_____

Employee Signature_____**Date**_____

Cc: Personnel File

71

The employee probably won't make comments and may not even take the memo. But it's your responsibility to offer a written reason when employment is terminated. By tracking the verbal and written warnings, you provide solid documentation in the termination memo as to why employment is terminated. Every employee deserves that.

Every employee, even the employee who does something so awful that employment has to be terminated without going through the discipline process. A good example would be the employee who is violent in the workplace. Whether or not you have a policy that prohibits violence in the workplace, it simply cannot be tolerated. Your other employees deserve to work in an environment free of violence and threats. Remember the discipline policy presented earlier in this chapter, it intentionally has a section that reads,

an employee may be suspended or dismissed immediately for any action that suggests that continued employment threatens another employee, the clients we serve, or would create an unfavorable working environment for other employees.

Don't suspend or terminate on the spot. Conduct an investigation and interview those who witnessed the action. Once you have your information, you can make your decision. If the violence did occur, then you have every right, as well as a responsibility to protect your other employees, to terminate employment. You can use the termination memo outlined earlier and it would read like this for this situation:

MEMO
TERMINATION OF EMPLOYMENT

TO: **Employee Name**

FROM: **Your Name**

DATE: **Date**

SUBJECT: **VIOLENCE IN THE WORKPLACE/EMPLOYMENT**
               TERMINATION

On DATE, it was brought to my attention that you threw a stack of papers over your cubicle at NAME OF OTHER EMPLOYEE. The stack of papers scattered and several hit NAME OF OTHER EMPLOYEE in the face. She, as well as another employee who witnessed the incident, have put the complaint in writing. After a full investigation, I have decided to terminate your employment. Violence, of any kind, will not be tolerated at COMPANY.

Employee Comments

_____

_____

_____

_____

_____

_____

_____

_____

Employee Signature_____**Date**_____

Witness Signature_____**Date**_____

Cc: Personnel File

It's probable that the employee won't sign the termination of employment memo so it's important to have a witness present to sign, stating that the conversation did take place.

Now let's discuss the situation when an employee *can't* do the job. And this is because s/he was not properly trained or does not have the tools needed to do the job. A *can't* situation may, at first, look like a *won't* situation. But once you've observed and listened, you should be able to make the distinction. Rather than discipline an employee who can't do the job, I like to develop a Plan of Action for that employee to follow. This allows the employee to get the training and/or tools needed to be successful in the job.

Let's consider the administrative assistant who consistently presents documents to you for your signature with typos, spelling errors, and grammar mistakes scattered throughout. And let's also assume that you have made it clear to this employee that when documents are presented for your signature, they are to be mailable (i.e., PERFECT).

PLAN OF ACTION

TO: Employee Name

FROM: Your Name

DATE: Date

SUBJECT: **JOB PERFORMANCE CHANGES NEEDED**

Current Behavior	Acceptable Behavior	Measurement	How to Get There	Time Table
Typos in documents	Documents are to be presented in mailable form free of typos	There will be no typos in documents that are presented as "finished"	Attend one day seminar on proofreading	Seminar is local on DATE. Attend that seminar. No typos after DATE will be tolerated; warning to follow.
Spelling errors in documents	Documents presented in mailable form free of typos	There will be no spelling errors in documents that are presented as "finished"	Set word processing program to ALWAYS display spelling errors	This can occur today. If you don't know how to set the default on your computer, call tech support.
Grammar mistakes in documents	Documents presented in mailable form free of grammar mistakes	There will be no grammar mistakes in documents that are presented as "finished"	Set word processing program to ALWAYS display improper grammar	This can occur today. If you don't know how to set the default on your computer, call tech support.

Employee Comments

_____

_____

_____

_____

_____

_____

_____

Employee Signature_____**Date**_____

Cc: Personnel File

This format can be altered to fit any job performance problem. In some cases, you'll even want to leave some of the table blank so your employee can have input in how the problems can be solved. This works. Every manager I've ever worked with who has used the Plan of Action method to correct job performance behaviors has thanked me. Jobs have been saved and an employee, who wants to do the right thing, has a plan to get there.

Providing day-to-day supervision for your employees is probably one of the most important responsibilities you have as a manager. Be a resource for them, be fair, and provide them with consistent supervision.

Chapter 6

How Are We Doing?

Every employee has the right to be evaluated on a regular basis. Whether or not your company has a formal program in place, YOU should have a formal program in place for every employee under your supervision. You owe them that. Every employee has a right to know how s/he is doing in his/her job. And every employee also has the right to know what you expect.

An employee who is new to the job may want to be evaluated frequently. Maybe using the formal evaluation process isn't the way to go if an employee wants to be evaluated every three months (or if you believe an employee needs to be evaluated every three months). But you should have something in place that allows you and the employee to sit down and discuss delivered performance and expectations on a schedule that both of you can agree upon. A new employee may need more frequent evaluation than an employee who has been on the job for a few years. Be flexible and give your employees performance expectations.

I also have a "no surprises" rule. This means that if you provide your employees with an annual evaluation of their performance, nothing in the formal evaluation can be a surprise. Everything you talk about and everything that is documented for the employee's file should simply be a confirmation of what you have talked about during the course of the year (or since the last performance evaluation). Most people like surprises, but not this kind. Don't let an employee hear for the first time that s/he's not meeting expectations after a year has gone by! Perhaps the performance could have been corrected if you'd only said something. And by not saying anything, you're actually saying that performance is good. You're validating that what the employee is doing on a day-to-day basis is just fine. Otherwise, you'd certainly say something about it,--that is what your employees are thinking.

So the annual evaluation should simply be a confirmation of what you've talked about during the year. No surprises.

Now I'm going to ask you to do something you may not have thought about before. Some companies are moving to or have already moved to this model. The company I work for has and it's proven to be very successful. Think for a moment about what it would be like to complete a performance evaluation without thinking about money. All you're going to do is evaluate performance without thinking, "If I rate him/her lower, I'll have to give him/her a smaller increase, and I know s/he needs the money. She's got a family and her son is off to college next year." Or, "I know s/he really tries hard and if I'm really honest, s/he won't get much of a raise. And I really like her." What you're doing is not telling your employee the truth! You're evaluating performance while you think about the employee's increase.

Let's separate pay from performance. Let's think just about performance. Let's go to a place where performance evaluations are just that—evaluations of performance. ONLY. That's what they're designed for. They're not designed to determine how much of an increase an employee should get. They're designed to help an employee live up to his/her potential and to meet the performance standards you've set.

Chapter 6
How Are We Doing?

They're designed to evaluate how well the employee has met performance standards as well as to set goals for the coming evaluation period. This is how well you've done. This is what you need to work on for the next period. Where does money come in? Is money the reward for doing what is expected in the first place? It shouldn't be. That's what the paycheck is for—paying for the job the employee was hired to do—and it's not a reward. A paycheck is just that—pay for work performed. A full day's work equals a full day's pay. It's not a reward. It's payment.

Think about the other things you pay for. You get your house painted. You agree on a price with the painter, your house gets painted, and you pay the bill. Do you give the painter MORE money because the house was painted to your specifications? NO. You simply pay the bill. If the house wasn't painted to your specifications, you ask to have the job fixed. And once the paint job meets your specifications, or the specifications you and the painter agreed upon, you pay the bill.

Just like with your employee. S/he agrees to do a job. S/he gets paid at the end of the week. Should this employee get more money during a week when s/he did great work? Should s/he get less money during a week when the work wasn't so great? No to both of those questions. Your employee will still get paid because that's what you agreed to when you made hiring decisions. And if the job isn't consistently performed to the expectations you've set, then you have either a training issue (can't do the job) or a disciplinary issue (won't do the job). But payment is still made.

81

A pay increase should address a bunch of other things. When an organization makes decisions about how much of an increase will be given during a particular year, the organization is thinking about a lot more than how well your employee does his/her job. The organization is looking at how much money it can put into pay increases, what the coming year looks like from a financial perspective, how much similar companies are giving for increases, what other companies in your industry are giving for pay increases, what can you afford, and probably a bunch of other things. So why, then, when you talk about an employee's performance, do you want to mess things up with pay increases! Truly, you don't! You want to keep the pay and increases separate.

Start thinking of the performance evaluation as a development tool for your employees. Start thinking of it as a way for your employees to discover how they can do better at the jobs they were hired to fill. Start thinking about what it would be like to work with employees who truly work toward improving their skills, not just because there is potentially more money at the end of the year, but because there is a desire to do so, because it is the right thing to do. Let your employee know that the paycheck will be there as long as the work is being done. An increase will be given because, among other things, the company *can*. Would the company give increases, no matter how good the work was performed, if it couldn't because of offshore competition or a year of significant losses? Probably not. And, based on a bunch of other factors (remember what we talked about earlier), this employee will make more money as s/he continues in the job.

82

Now, most of those other factors will be decisions made by your upper management group. When your organization determines what it can afford to put into pay increases, it will look at what business looks like for the coming year. This is called forecasting. If business looks good, maybe your organization will put additional money into pay increases. Your company will also look at what its competitors are doing and it will have a general sense of what similar companies are doing in terms of pay increases. You, as a manager, can't really be concerned with any of that. You'll be told, probably, that you have a certain amount of money for pay increases and that it's up to you how you'd like to distribute that money.

You're going to think of all of the employees who report to you and, whether you admit it or not, you're going to do something that some employees won't like. And you'll be able to guess which ones won't like what you're going to do. Think about this a minute. Think about all the employees in your department. Think of your star performers—those employees who routinely go above and beyond what you expect of them, the employees who, when you have to depend on someone, you think of them. Think of your employees who do their jobs every day, meet your expectations, and are good employees. Now think of your employees who are probably marginal. They do their work but they never go out of their way to help another department employee. They go through the motions of their jobs without going one step further. They get by. Quite frankly, if any of those employees left the organization, you really wouldn't miss them.

Admit it. You've just ranked every employee in your department! And employees in the bottom third HATE it when you do that. They probably know that you do that. But they're not willing to move up to the middle third rank because it would require effort on their part. The employees in the top third know you rank them, too. And, they're thrilled that you do that. They know they're up there. They work hard to maintain that rank. They stand out from the rest of your employees. They WANT to stand out.

Now, do you think the employees you've just ranked in the top third actually work that hard, every day, because they may get an additional percent of increase next year? Do you really think that those employees in the top tier work harder than the rest because there is some type of minimal additional increase at the end of the year? Do you think that's why those employees put out the extra effort each and every day? Nope. Whether they get 3% or 4% or 5% at the end of the year, they'll still give you extra. Every day.

And you don't need a performance evaluation tool to tell you who your best employees are. And you don't need a performance evaluation tool to tell you who your marginal employees are. You already know that and you haven't even filled out one piece of paper.

So, why then, do you continue to tie performance evaluations to pay increases? It just doesn't make any sense to base the increase only on that. Let's be radical and move to considering the performance evaluation process as a tool to be used in the development of employees. Because that's what it was designed to do. And if you want to, take your ranked list of employees and tie that, along with all of those other factors (external market conditions, company's profitability, and internal equity which we'll discuss in a minute) to pay increases. Keep the performance evaluation tool out of and let it do what it was designed to do—evaluate the past year's performance and set goals for the coming year. It's okay to give higher increases to the star performers, but it's not the only reason to give an increase. It's simply a piece of the performance evaluation pie. If you give increases based solely on performance, and you make it known that this is how your company does it, then in a bad year, you'll have to admit that even though performance was exceptional, the company just doesn't have any money for increases. What a let down. . .and when I tried so hard. Don't set your employees up for disappointment.

Now, let's take this one step further. If you're currently awarding pay increases when you conduct the annual performance evaluation, then you're not really ranking your employees. And that's something you want to do. You do it already so just admit it. But, by giving pay increases throughout the year, probably on anniversary date, you don't take into consideration internal equity. How can you?! How can you look at Sally's pay and compare her pay to Ben's pay when Ben isn't even due for his performance evaluation for five months? They're not on the same calendar so Sally is either always going to be five months behind or seven months ahead of Ben. Again, this doesn't make any sense.

Consider moving all of your pay increases to the same time every year. That way, your ranking system will make sense. You'll be forced to look at internal equity. You'll be forced to consider not only the performance evaluation, but all of those other things. Sure, the performance evaluation has a place in determining a pay increase, but you already know who's doing a great job and who's not. The evaluation is, again, simply a tool to help your employees. Look at your department as a whole, rank the stars on down the line, look at who is making what and decide if the ranking matches the pay scale. And if it doesn't you know what you have to do. You may not be able to accomplish the task in one year, but you can put a plan in place for the next several years.

By separating the performance evaluation from the annual increase and giving increases at one time during the year, you consider performance, along with everything else you must consider. And this makes sense. For your department and for your company. There is too much at stake when you use JUST the performance evaluation to determine a pay increase. You can't be completely honest. But when it's just a part of the process, well, this makes sense. Finally!

Let's look at the performance evaluation tool itself. Your organization may or may not have one in place. If you have one in place, get out a sample copy. Now.

In my over 20 years as a HR professional, I've found that most employees like to have a say in how their performance is evaluated. And when you think about this, your employees probably want this too. They probably don't prefer to sit quietly while you "deliver" their performance evaluations. Probably they have comments about their performance or, more accurately, comments about YOUR evaluation of their performance.

Think about the last performance evaluation you did. Your employee probably made some comments about either past performance or future goals. Your employee was participating in his/her performance evaluation. Maybe not formally, but s/he was certainly participating. Even if s/he just agreed and/or disagreed with comments you were making, there was participation going on. Employees like to participate. So, let's give them the opportunity to do it formally, as part of the record!

What I'm talking about here is Self Evaluation. And this can be an intimidating experience for an employee who has never done it "formally." Yes, they currently do it because they are making comments about their own performance. But it's not "formal." They don't currently fill out a form. They just talk. Let's give them some ownership here and give them the opportunity to participate in their own performance development. What a concept! An employee participating in his/her job development. Rather than you, as the manager, just saying this and that about performance, you're going to take the employee's comments and think about them. Your comments are really just your perceptions. See what your employee has to say. Don't just "deliver" the performance evaluation. Let your employee have his/her say, too. Let your employee participate. After all, it's his/her performance both of you are talking about. How can you, as the manager, have all of the answers. You don't DO the job. You just observe your employee doing the job. Find out what s/he thinks about how well s/he is doing. In other words, take a walk in your employee's shoes. Try them on. See how they fit.

Okay. This may sound like a lot of work. Especially if your company doesn't have a human resources department to develop this type of program. Not to worry. Just use the form you're already using to evaluate performance and let your employee fill it out, too. Let your employee "play manager" and complete the form and evaluate his/her own performance. And then swap forms. Don't ask your employee to complete the form and then look at it before you complete your form! Complete them separately and then swap forms. Take a few days to really think about what each of you has to say about this employee's performance. Then meet to discuss performance together. You've both evaluated this employee's performance independently and you know what each other thinks. Now, talk about it. Both forms together make up the annual performance evaluation and both forms become part of the employee's personnel file.

Talk about how this employee did last year and understand how s/he thinks s/he did last year. Discuss goals for the coming year TOGETHER. Write a plan together for this employee for the entire year so s/he can improve or perfect his/her performance. By having this employee involved in the evaluation of his/her performance, you give this employee ownership. Put together a timetable and visit it regularly. Remember those supervision sessions? Now you have something concrete to talk about. You can talk about performance AND goals. You are truly helping your employee develop to his/her full potential when you allow participation in the job. Your employee isn't any longer just doing the job, s/he is participating in his/her own development.

Maybe you've identified training that could help this employee improve performance. Let the employee investigate what is available and come to you with a plan for attending the training. Maybe you've identified performance behaviors that need to be modified. Talk about how s/he is doing each time you meet. Pull the evaluation form out and talk about the sections the employee is working on. Talk about progress. Talk about goals. Talk about the past and talk about the future. And LISTEN. Listen to what your employee is saying about his/her performance. And you'll notice that, once your employee is actively participating in his/her job, the work improves (if it needed to) or it gets even better (it can ALWAYS get better) or the employee's attitude improves or IT gets even better. You're helping to develop leaders in those employees who want to lead because you've helped them identify that that's what they want to do.

Now you're a REAL manager. And you're ready to help those employees who have the desire to move up the promotion ladder.

Hey, did you happen to notice that this employee was honest about his/her performance? Could it be because what s/he said didn't make or break the raise?

Chapter 7

Going Up

Everyone knows that there are stars in every company. Your company is no different. Many organizations, yours again is no different, probably look at the stars in your company and think, "Wow, I've got my next manager candidate because this employee is so good at turfting." Remember the Promotion Fairy? Well, she's baaaaaaaack!

She's knocking but don't let her in your office! She thinks that everyone who is good at trufting ought to be a manager. That's how SHE got to be a manager. She was great at ploarting and now she's the Promotion Fairy. Lock her out. Don't let her in your department. She can't see that employees who are good at turfting are happy turfting. She only sees them as future managers because of the turfting. Hey, Promotion Fairy. . .ever heard of Performance Promotion Ladders?

No. Unfortunately, she hasn't. All she knows is that if your organization has good employees doing some great turfting, well then, they should be managing other turfting employees You've got to keep her out of your department. And you've got to keep your employees who are great turfters, continuing to turft, but not necessarily managing other turfters. There's a lot to be said for allowing an employee to master a skill, enjoy doing that skill, and then letting that employee continue to practice that skill.

Let's explore the concept of Performance Promotion Ladders. Why is it that companies take employees who are really good at something and try to turn them into something else? Why do companies think it makes sense to take employees out of jobs they're really good at and put them into positions (management) they have no experience in and maybe no desire for? How can you possibly evaluate an employee's potential as a manager when that employee is simply a goof turfter? Why not consider keeping that employee who is really good at turfting, turfting? How can you do that? If I don't eventually promote her into management, well, she'll leave. Consider a Performance Promotion Ladder.

I'm not saying that an employee who has turfted for a certain number of years should automatically be promoted to the next level (read: "Civil Service" here). What I am saying is that when an employee has mastered a certain skill level and is moving into the next skill level, consider moving this employee up the Performance Promotion Ladder. Don't make an employee feel that, in order to move up within the organization, s/he has to move into management. Put this Performance Promotion Ladder in place in your department so that employees can move up within their jobs without having to move out into a management position. If you're forcing employees into management in order to be promoted, you're sending the message: Management is more important than the work you are doing. If you want to get ahead, you'll have to go into management. No matter that you're a great turfter. If you want a promotion, you'll have to supervise other turfters. Your work isn't really important. The management of the work, however, is.

It's not unusual in the organizations I've worked with to have managers actually making LESS than some of the employees under their supervision. What? You've never heard of this before? Well hear it now. It makes sense. Especially in highly specialized or technical areas. My feeling is that if you're a good manager, you can probably manage anyone, doing anything, for any organization. (I think I'm a good manager and I've held human resources management positions in a bunch of different industries: restaurant, mental health, health care, financial services, software development, data management, retail chain.) But, if you have employees who have mastered a particular skill, why would you want to move them out in order to move them up? Let them stay right where they are. Let them make good money, maybe more money than you make, when they do their jobs well. Stop making them think they have to move out of a job to move up in the organization. They don't. And you're weakening your department when you have this kind of practice in place.

So, recognize your employees who have mastered certain skills. Develop a Performance Promotion Ladder. Make it relevant for your department. It can look something like this when you tailor make it for your department's function.

Position Title	Skills Mastered
Customer Service Trainee	**Consistently delivers exceptionally high customer service as evidenced by:**
Customer Service Representative	**Has mastered Customer Service Trainee skills AND provides support and guidance to other team members by:**
Customer Service Account Executive	**Has mastered Customer Service Trainee and Customer Service Representative skills AND is able to escalate customer service queries by:**
Customer Service Executive	**Has mastered Customer Service Trainee, Representative and Account Executive skills AND provides training to new employees and to those new to their skill level.**

Not every customer service employee will be hired as a Customer Service Trainee. You may hire individuals at any level, depending on prior relevant experience, providing they have mastered the Skills Mastered requirements. What's important to remember is that you shouldn't force employees who are good at what they do into management positions in order to better themselves within the organization. Show your employees that you value the work that they do and that there is value in their jobs. You can do this by developing Performance Promotion Ladders within your department.

But let's say that you have a position open within your department and either nobody is ready for the next step up the ladder, many are ready for the next step up the ladder, or it's a new position. When this is the case, you should post the position within the organization and you may decide to advertise the position externally as well. By posting the position, you invite current employees to apply, whether already in your department or from another department, and you invite external candidates as well.

When you have a position open that several candidates qualify for, you alleviate having to "tap someone on the shoulder" and possibly be accused of showing favoritism (or even worse, discrimination). You invite all interested qualified candidates to apply for the position. There may be some employees who qualify but aren't interested; they may think they're not ready for the next step. By doing this, you give employees the option of applying or not.

It's a good practice to interview internal and external candidates at the same time and NEVER to say that you'll always hire the internal candidate over an external candidate. That won't always happen. There may be times when you do, in fact, hire an external candidate over an internal candidate. Remember how we discussed "fit" in an earlier chapter. Well, that applies here too. An external candidate may be a better fit when you need to breathe new life into your department, when you feel like an outside perspective is needed in order to revitalize the department, or when you have several internal candidates who are almost ready for a step up the ladder but aren't quite there yet. Always practice (and publicize this practice) hiring and promoting the "best fit."

Posting open positions also encourages employees within other departments to move around internally. Some job changes may be lateral steps (i.e., not a promotion up the ladder but a move sideways that is not accompanied by a pay increase) for internal candidates. Whether an internal candidate is from within your department or from another department, it's a good practice to always interview all internal candidates. Even if, after reviewing qualifications, you determine that the internal candidate does not meet the Rule of Minimums, it's a great opportunity for you to do some job counseling and to get to know another employee a little better, to explore the employee's goals, and to determine if maybe this employee could fill another position in the future. Never let this type of opportunity pass you by.

It's good to encourage movement within an organization, and some departments are even seen as "entry level departments" to the organization. If that's your department, don't consider it a liability. Yours is the department door that most people must enter in order to work for the organization. Employees who know they have advancement opportunities within an organization tend to be more productive, happier employees because they don't consider themselves in dead-end jobs.

Consider whether or not you want to put a practice in place where employees must stay in current jobs a minimum amount of time, maybe six months to a year. In doing so, an employee who might be a good fit for a promotion could lose out because the time requirement has not been met. But the other side of this is that when you put this practice in place, you're telling employees that you think they need to be in their jobs a certain amount of time, in order to learn the job and to give the job a fair chance, before moving on, either to another job in your department or to another department all together. And, by doing this, you are assured that the training you provide is used well and that someone new to a job doesn't move on before you get to take advantage of the skills you've taught.

In order to get the best of both sides, you could put this practice in place with the caveat that it is a *guideline*, not a hard and fast rule, and that your organization believes that in the best interest of the employee and the company, an employee should stay in a job a certain minimum amount of time. However, at the discretion of management, this practice may not be followed when it is believed to be in the best interest of the organization and the employee.

Now you have to determine how you'll handle the money-end of a promotion. If your organization is sophisticated enough to have a wage and salary program in place, you can use that scale. If you don't have a program in place, and you're faced with a promotion, put the salaries of everyone in the department in front of you and identify everyone doing a job similar to the one you've just promoted another employee into. See where that employee fits in terms of pay and adjust that employee's pay accordingly, based on the internal equity of those currently doing the job. Take into consideration how long current employees have been doing the work and adjust the pay of the newcomer appropriately. A good rule of thumb might be to adjust down three percent for each year the newcomer has not done the job, compared with someone who has been in the job up to five years. After five years, it probably doesn't make sense to adjust down any further due to inflation and market conditions. Just have this pay increase in mind BEFORE you talk about the promotion. Don't leave it until the end because the employee could turn you down. Talk about money first, get it out of the way, and then talk about the promotion. The pay increase is just what it is and should not be negotiated. And if you've done your homework (like when you're offering a candidate a job once the interview process is completed), you'll be prepared.

You could also have a practice in place where promotions equal a certain percentage of pay as an increase. It could be a flat 5-15 percent increase for a promotion up one step of the ladder. But don't get yourself into a position of having to negotiate the pay increase once the candidate has been identified, has shown interest, and you're ready to move him/her up. Get the money end of the promotion out of the way first. During the interview talk about the pay increase and get it behind you. If you leave it until the end, you risk having the promotion turned down because it's not enough of an increase for the increased workload or because the employee had higher expectations than the organization can meet. You've wasted your time and the employee's time. And be prepared that some employees will not be interested in a promotion—they like what they're doing, they're good at it, and they don't want the increased responsibility. Accept that and move on. Don't put yourself in the position of trying to convince someone that s/he's ready to move up. It's usually a mistake, both for the organization and for the employee who believes s/he is not ready. And if an hourly employee is faced with a promotion into a salaried position, it could represent a decrease in total compensation because of increased workload, increased hours, and no pay for overtime.

Chapter 8

Tick Tock. . .We're Watching the Clock

There are oodles of books about time management and there are just as many time management "systems." I will not devote the time (no pun intended. . .well, just a little; I couldn't resist) in this chapter to a subject that deserves to be explored in depth. But I will give you some guidance and practical skills you can use and share with your employees so that they can start to practice good time management.

Rule One: Do like tasks together. This may sound like just good old common sense. And it is. But few employees really practice Rule One. The administrative assistant again. S/he returns a few email messages, makes a phone call, types a document, returns a voice mail message, types the envelope to go with the document, gets a cup of tea, catches up with his/her boss, starts to sort the mail, answers the phone, and on and on. At first glance you may mistake the above for a normal start of the day. And, you may even applaud this employee because it's clear that s/he can multi-task—a highly coveted skill.

But look closer. This isn't really multi-tasking. It's wasting time. By restructuring the beginning of the day just slightly, this employee can get these tasks completed in less time and more efficiently because s/he won't be jumping from task to task.

The best way I know of to actually get a handle on this employee's job is to ask him/her to complete a time study. At first, you'll be met with a fair amount of resistance. (Why do you want to know how I spend my day? Do you plan to get rid of me? Do you think I waste time? Well, why don't you do my job for a day! See how YOU like it!) But let your employee know that you'll be reviewing the time study in order to help him/her manage the day better. This will reduce the feeling of helplessness and, consequently, this employee should feel less stressed.

A typical time study log will look like this:

Time Started	Tasks	Interruptions	Time Completed	Notes
800-815				
815-830				
830-845				
845-900				
900-915				
915-930				
930-945				
945-1000				
1000-1015				
1015-1030				
1030-1045				
1045-1100				
1100-1115				
1115-1130				
1130-1145				
1145-1200				

By structuring the log in this TIME format rather than by TASK, you'll get a good picture of what exactly this employee is doing. I also suggest doing it in 15-minute increments. When you review this log with your employee, you can talk about why, when s/he started opening and sorting the mail at 900, that task didn't actually get done until 1100. Talk about the interruptions (this is a very important column and will provide lively discussion) and how you can help this employee avoid distraction, if that's the case, or simply how to avoid interruptions. Certainly, answering the phone is not an interruption, but another employee who stops by to chat several times throughout the morning *is*. You may also find that YOU are a distraction AND an interruption. Remember the supervision sessions. Another advantage of having regularly scheduled meetings with your employee is that you can avoid countless interruptions throughout the day. Meet once in the morning to outline the day's work, maybe once during the day and perhaps at the end of the day to discuss the next day's work. Quit stopping by and interrupting your employee. Can't you see s/he's working!

When you help your employee to group "like" tasks together, you help him/her to organize and plan the day more efficiently. By helping this employee to structure his/her day so that all 15 email messages are read, dealt with, and answered between 900-1000, and again between 400-500, you help him/her to allow him/herself the permission to NOT answer email messages throughout the day. Let's be honest, a good many email messages are "forwards" that are relatively meaningless, cute sayings and office jokes, scattered among business-related messages. By structuring the day with an hour to deal with emails in the morning and again in the afternoon, this employee will be forced to simply get rid of the ones that have little, if any, business reason for existence. And s/he'll find him/herself on a roll answering emails, rather than doing it sporadically. Others in the office will, hopefully, stop sending "cute sayings" that demand a reply because a reply won't be forthcoming. Everyone is a lot happier at work minus the emails from others who don't have enough to do!

I've found that in this not-so-new high tech world, companies tend to be one of the following: email, voice mail, or walk-down-the-hall kinds of companies. And there are advantages that come with each type of company. But whether your employees email, voice mail, or take a stroll, these types of tasks should be grouped together. It probably makes sense to structure this employee's day so that voice mail messages are listened to at the beginning of the day (could be something important that needs to be dealt with right off) and then a few times more throughout the day. However, that does NOT mean that each voice mail message needs to be returned promptly. Important ones should definitely be returned. But most can probably adhere to Rule One: Do Like Tasks Together. It makes more sense, it takes less time, and makes for a more pleasant day because work will get DONE.

Just before it's time to go home, it's a good idea to help your employee summarize today and prepare for tomorrow. This is Rule Two: Summarize and Prep. S/he will review everything that didn't get done today because this is the beginning of tomorrow's work. Leftover work may not be the highest priority, but it does need to be bumped to tomorrow. By taking a few minutes at the end of the day (not more than 15; a pro can do this in five minutes or less) to prepare for tomorrow, a sense of accomplishment is achieved for what was completed, and a task list is built for what was not. By writing down tasks, you help your employee to stop thinking about them. S/he will check off tasks as they are completed (voice mail messages returned and handled, email messages answered and dealt with, person-to-person exchanges either done or not) and move to tomorrow's tasks.

What happens to a task that is not moved to tomorrow? One of two things: it's either forgotten about (this is not good) or it's dwelled on until it is done (this is even worse and it could ruin an otherwise restful evening, weekend, or vacation). Summarize and Prep by WRITING THINGS DOWN. Once tasks are recorded on paper, the employee can think about something else, accomplish something else, or just enjoy the time not thinking about what didn't get done today.

Rule Three: Keep a Task Journal. THIS is where your employee will write things down. No, not on post it notes left affixed to his/her computer screen (they're in the way here) or on scraps of paper on a pointy spindle (they don't get looked at once they're speared) or shoved into a file (never to see the light of day again). This journal doesn't have to be anything fancy. It can be a three-ring binder, a spiral-bound notebook, even a calendar desk blotter with lined spaces for tasks. Or it can be a computer program like Microsoft Outlook or even an on-line Internet service provider, like AOL. There are lots of options, high tech, low tech, and no tech.

The important thing is that Rule Three be kept. Then you can move on to Rule Four: Refer to the Task Journal Throughout the Day. This is really time management at its best because your employee is managing his/her time rather than having time manage him/her. There is a lot of satisfaction to be had from simply checking off a task in the Task Journal. And there is also a record of the task, the task being accomplished, and notes about that task. A page in the Journal could be set up like this:

December 27

Priority 1, 2, 3	Task	Important Notes	Date Completed	Moved
2	Schedule meeting with Sam and Sharon to discuss Quarterly Staff Meeting	Sam can't be involved; Sharon and I will meet on January 7 at 3:00.	January 3	
3	Type letter to Chamber of Commerce for Deb's signature	She wants marketing folders included with all letters; order large envelopes		To January 5
1	Pick up George at airport 3:00 on January 13	Put in calendar for January 13	January 6	

Of course, you can help your employee to set up his/her Task Journal any way that seems to make sense for the particular job s/he is doing. This Task Journal is a valuable tool to help your employee manage his/her time. If s/he will be using a three-ring binder, notebook paper will work beautifully. This Task Journal can accompany the employee to his/her regularly scheduled supervision sessions with you so you can talk about what has been accomplished as well as add tasks that need to be accomplished, along with priorities and deadlines. (I told you I'd make this easy!) A binder clip can be used as a place marker. Keep all old pages for future reference.

You might also ask your employee to highlight tasks that need to be discussed during the regular supervision session. If something was not accomplished, have him/her highlight it with comments noting why.

Once your employee gets in the habit of writing things down, Rule Three, s/he will find that the day goes much more smoothly, there is a great sense of accomplishment at the end of the day, and having a record of work accomplished and work that needs to be accomplished provides for stimulating supervision sessions. Your employee will find that s/he is more productive when s/he discovers, that by following these four rules, s/he is taking ownership of his/her job, not simply doing work.

And we've come full circle because taking ownership of one's job is the key to high productivity, personal satisfaction, and effective time management.

Chapter 9

Kickin' Butt

Just like real people, employees prefer to do things they ENJOY doing. Imagine that. You have employees who would prefer to do work they enjoy rather than doing work they don't enjoy. Just like real people. There are two kinds of people. Yep. Just TWO. The first kind of person does what s/he likes to do first. I've found that this person, let's call this person Leftover Louie, not only does what he likes to do first in terms of work, but watch this person eat a meal. He eats the good stuff first. The theory is that, "If I get full, then I won't have to eat the stuff I don't like." Same with work. "If I get to the end of the day, and I'm not done with all of my tasks, well, I won't have to do the stuff I don't like to do."

Then there's Finishit Frannie. She gets all the work that she dreads done first. That way she has it behind her and she can get on to the fun stuff. Every company wants to hire Finishit Frannie. Some people may call Frannie hyper. She's just a whirling dervish. Trouble is, there just aren't enough Frannies to go around. Ever have lunch with Frannie? She knows she should eat a balanced lunch every day, but, unfortunately she's just not fond of vegetables. But Frannie, resourceful as she is, found a way to eat a balanced meal. She drinks vegetable juice with her lunch and she's half way to meeting her daily requirements before the day's half over. This is the same way Frannie tackles the dreaded filing that is a part of her job. She gets it done first. Right when she walks in the door. It's done for the day and then she doesn't have to think about it anymore.

But there aren't many Finishit Frannies looking for work. There are lots of Leftover Louies, though. So, the way I've helped employees solved this problem, is the same way I helped my children with this very same issue. Kids like to eat all the good stuff first. In fact, the phrase, "eat dessert first," was written by a child. Probably by one of my children. By eating all the good stuff first, the yucky stuff doesn't get eaten because "Mom, dinner was great, but I can't finish my brussel sprouts, I'm stuffed" becomes a common lament. Thinking the brussel sprouts would be headed for the compost bin, my child thinks dinner is over. And it is. But the sprouts are "saved" for another time, like the next meal. Yum, brussel sprouts for breakfast. My kids are teenagers now. Erin actually likes most vegetables and we fight over leftover broccoli (yes, really). Brad, however, is not fond of most vegetables. He's even less fond of leftover broccoli for breakfast. So he eats it by just about swallowing it whole and washing it down with a quart of milk. I think I've even seen him dunk broccoli. And he enjoys Cheerios for breakfast. He learned early.

This same tactic can be used at work with tasks that are equally as yucky. (I happen to love brussel sprouts, by the way.) If the filing doesn't get done by the end of the day, then it's the first thing the employee faces tomorrow. No exceptions. The work is still there (as are the sprouts) facing the employee (or the child).

Let's face it. Every job has parts to it that are not exactly enjoyable. But all of those parts do have to be done. Help your employees understand that once the boring tasks are accomplished, the more interesting work can be tackled. You have an opportunity here to be a good role model. Use yourself as an example and talk about the parts of your job that you don't find particularly stimulating. Talk about how you accomplish those tasks and help your employee to use similar tactics to complete his/her own tasks.

Employees are motivated more easily to do work they enjoy and are good at than work they consider boring or aren't good at. In fact, you probably won't even have to motivate your employees to do the work they enjoy. The battle will be in helping them find ways to make even the most mundane work accomplishable. Sometimes the work just has to be "worked through" and gotten done. Get the boring stuff, or the brussel sprouts, out of the way and move on!

Now, that's the answer for some employees. Other employees may do better by doing the mundane work at the end of the workday, when their energy level is low. As long as Leftover Louie knows that at the end of the day he'll be facing the work he finds particularly unappealing, he may be fine with that. But he has to realize that the work must be done. And it must be done by *him*. Whether it's at the end of the day when his energy is low or he's finishing up yesterday's work the following day, it HAS TO BE DONE. You'll spend some time following up with LL to make sure the work does get done. This is supervision. And, really, what do you care *when* it gets done, as long as it *does* get done in a reasonable amount of time.

Talk to your employees and determine with them how they work best. Do you have a bunch of Finishit Frannies or several Leftover Louies? Help them recognize their high and low energy periods and help them organize their work to best take advantage of their energy levels. Talk to your employees. Be a role model for them and help them to get through the brussel sprouts daily!

Chapter 10

Did Not. . .Did Too!

If your goal is to eliminate conflict from your work environment, you've set yourself up for failure. Conflict exists everywhere. Once you admit that you'll be able to view it positively and use it constructively. Conflict is good.

Conflict occurs when two or more people view something differently. The more passionate we feel about a particular issue, the more potential conflict there is with someone who doesn't share that view.

Conflict in the workplace can be a very positive force when you allow your employees to voice their opinions. Anytime you encourage one employee to try "their" way of doing something, which may be very different from the way that something has always been done, you're inviting conflict. You'll hear things from other employees like, well, that's the way we've always done that. Translation: Hey, it's easy to do it that way, we've always done it that way and, well, that's the way it's done. Why make this any harder than it already is? Good question. But if you don't allow, even encourage, that exploration, you may never find that there's an even better way of doing something.

Sometimes, however, conflict can get out of hand. It can become a negative force in your department. Therefore, it's up to you, as the manager, to set the tone: Conflict is good when we use it to explore new ways of doing things, to go where no man has gone before, to seek out new worlds (raise your hand if you're a Trekkie). Be the conflict poster child by allowing it, nurturing it, and, when necessary, mediating it.

Yes, you'll be the mediator. Because conflict, as good as it can be, can also be in excess. Too much of anything--chocolate, fried food, pastries, even conflict--is not good. If you allow it, conflict can take over your department just like fried food can take over your waistline. So, like good, expensive chocolate or a cherry cream cheese popover, have just a little, enjoy what it does for you, enjoy how it makes you feel, and then move on. And, if you've eaten dessert first, you could be heading for a forkful of brussel sprouts!

As a manager, you'll at some point find yourself in a position to mediate conflict between two employees. You'll know that you need to get involved either because one of them has requested your intervention or because you've experienced tension in the department or an interruption in the workflow. Don't be naive and think that if you wait long enough the situation will resolve itself. It rarely does. In fact, it will probably get worse. Step right in there, confront the individuals, listen to the issues, help them resolve it, and get back to work.

That sounds easy. But good confrontation skills don't usually come easily to managers. Human nature dictates that we avoid conflict. The "fight or flight" instinct surfaces and most of us would choose "flight." Develop your conflict resolution skills and help your employees resolve their conflict. Be a good role model and let your employees see how it's done.

What to do then? When you're faced with resolving a conflict between two co-workers, you'll be the mediator. As mediator, your role is to find the truth. You'll make no accusations, you'll express no opinion, and you'll not take sides. You'll listen and you'll help your employees listen to one another.

Good listeners take responsibility for what they say and how they feel. To help your employees develop good listening skills, you need to exhibit this behavior yourself. Remember, you're the role model. Let's look at a typical workplace situation.

Clem is a member of the customer service team. It's important that at least five individuals are answering phones at all times. There are eight people on the team so breaks, starting times, and ending times are all staggered. Clem has worked for the company for about six months and is doing a great job. However, in the last few weeks, you've noticed that he's been arriving anywhere between 10 and 15 minutes late in the morning. This puts a strain on the other team members because mornings tend to be particularly busy. Clem has a very strong personality and you've been avoiding "the talk" with him. You hate to confront employees, even when they're doing something wrong. It's much easier to just look the other way and hope that *it* goes away. Whatever *it* is.

But several employees have complained to you about Clem's tardiness this past week. They don't think it's fair that they have to keep covering for him so they've blown his cover. You act surprised and promise that you'll address this with Clem by the end of the week.

Well, it's Friday and it's happened one more time since the two employees approached you. It's time to have that talk with Clem.

How should you approach this with Clem? You certainly don't look forward to his confrontational nature and it's important for you to not be on the defensive. After all, you are the manager and you need to start managing Clem.

The first mistake you made was not addressing the situation right when you became aware of it. When we let work habits continue, we are, in fact, condoning the behavior. We're saying, without saying it, that this is good. And Clem probably believes that it's just no big deal since you haven't mentioned it.

Before speaking with Clem, do your homework. If your company has a policy on punctuality, get it out. You may also have operations procedures for your department. Read them and note areas of importance that include providing exceptional customer service, punctuality, courtesy, and professionalism.

Now, decide how you will approach Clem. You need to focus on the effect his tardiness is having on department operations, employee morale, and his own professionalism. If confrontation is difficult for you, script your conversation so that you have a good idea of how the conversation should progress.

You don't want to fall into the trap of blaming Clem for something that he may have no control over. After all, you don't know why he's been late. But why is not the issue. Focus your statements on his behavior, not on him personally or on his

114

personal life. Talk only of Clem's job performance behaviors and your company's work standards, not about Clem. Talk about how his behavior is affecting the operations of the department. Some of your statements could include the following:

Clem, I've reviewed your timecards and found that you've been late clocking in six times over the last three weeks. This is a fact that would be hard to dispute.

When you're late for work, other employees are forced to answer your phone lines, in order for us to continue to provide the exceptional customer service this department is known for. This is another indisputable fact.

Now, without asking Clem why, put him in a position to explain how his needs may have changed since he took the position. *Clem, when I interviewed you over six months ago, we talked at length about the rigorous schedule requirements for the person filling the position and the fact that the company could offer almost no schedule flexibility. Do you remember that part of the interview?*

It's important that every employee meet the demands of the schedule. I understand your needs may have changed since you accepted the position. Do you feel like this position is still a good fit for you? You're putting Clem in the position of making a decision here: will he stay or will he go? He knows if he stays, he's making a schedule commitment. Ultimately, the choice is his and the conflict is resolved.

When you confront an employee about job performance behaviors and standards, you must never fall into attack mode. Everything you say needs to focus on the facts. Keep your emotions out of it. Don't talk about being "let down" or "disappointed" when an employee fails to meet your expectations. Talk about the job, the requirements of the job, and your expectations for how the job should be performed. Give the employee a choice to either meet the requirements of the job, and, therefore, fulfill expectations, or to find a job that is a better fit. When you present the conflict and focus on facts, job performance behaviors, and expectations, you force the employee to own up and make a choice.

Let's look at another approach to managing conflict. This is called the "When you. . .I feel. . .because. . ." approach to conflict resolution, or WYIFB. This approach works well for employees who are experiencing conflict with one another. And, as the manager, you can help them to develop skills to manage the conflict between them.

Meet Kathryn and Pete. They share a cubicle. They share a job. They share paperclips, scissors, and a computer. What they don't share is a definition of the word, "tidy." Kathryn works mornings and Pete works afternoons. Kathryn is a great employee. She produces a phenomenal amount of very high quality work. She's efficient, uses her time well, and is a great fit for her job.

Alas, Kathryn is also a slob. She eats breakfast at her desk, leaving a trail of crumbs behind her. She's constantly snacking on granola, and fruit. Apples, strawberries, pears, whatever happens to be in season. Kathryn is always munching. But that doesn't stop her productivity. She seems to work best with a bowl of something at hand. It's a wonder she doesn't pop an eraser instead of a berry. By the time she goes home, her wastebasket is filled with empty juice cans, apple cores, peanut shells, and a yogurt container or two. It's a good thing the trash is emptied daily.

Pete is tidy. Paperclips go here, the stapler goes there. An extra ream of paper for the printer goes here, ink cartridges there. Pete doesn't eat at his desk but he has a water bottle going at all times. Covered, of course. No water spills on this keyboard. No snacking for Pete. He eats his regular three meals a day and will have an afternoon snack—in the break room.

After sharing a job for just over a month, Pete asks for a private meeting with you. You anticipate that he'll talk about how the job-share is working. Guess again. Pete comes to you with a list of complaints—all about Kathryn. He's the first one to admit that she's great at what she does. But he doesn't know if he can live like this anymore. The job-share is great and allows him to continue with his education. But there's dots of apple juice on the monitor, paperclips in the rubber band container, and a wastebasket full of cores when he assumes his post in the afternoons. He knows he can't duplicate this arrangement with any other company. But he can't continue like this. "She cleans up her act, or I'm outta here. You'll have my two-week notice tomorrow," Pete announces reluctantly.

You convince Pete to stay, promising him that you'll talk with Kathryn tomorrow morning, first thing. No, Pete decides. He doesn't think you should do his dirty work. He's in the middle of Introduction to Psychology and he'd like to give this confrontation thing a test run. But, to be honest, he's just a little scared of Kathryn.

117

"She scares me." He tells you. "She's great at what she does, but I haven't mentioned this to her because I'm afraid she'll yell at me." Pete doesn't like it when voices are raised.

As their manager, it's up to you to help Pete develop conflict resolution skills so that he can handle this situation on his own.

The first thing you do is help Pete outline what he wants to discuss. Since Kathryn's work is first-rate, all he really wants to address is her slovenly ways. You suggest he use the WYIFB approach.

Pete makes a list of the behaviors he'd like Kathryn to change.

No eating at our desk.

No tossing empty containers in our trash—take them to the break room trash.

No mixing paperclips and rubber bands.

Then you ask Pete to talk about how he feels when Kathryn behaves in this manner.

"Kathryn, when you leave our desk messy, I feel like I have to clean up after you before I begin working because I can't work in that type of environment."

You are helping Pete to take responsibility for his feelings, and you agree with him that Kathryn needs to be more responsible in this job-share arrangement. You help Pete manage his feelings so that he can help Kathryn manage her behavior. He's not accusing Kathryn. It's indisputable that she leaves the desk messy. She would probably agree to that. By using the word, "messy" Pete is confronting the behavior. If Pete used "a slob" in describing Kathryn instead of the work environment, he'd be attacking Kathryn and the conversation would be over.

Pete is stating that he has to clean up before he can start working. Again, this is Pete talking about Pete. It's hard to dispute someone's personal feelings. Kathryn can't tell him that he can't feel a certain way. And the fact that he can't work in that environment is also indisputable. Pete is giving Kathryn an opportunity to tidy up so that he can be productive. The more productive Pete is, the better off Kathryn will be because the job will truly be shared. If Kathryn continues to be a slob, Pete will spend part of his time on the job cleaning up after her and then she will be forced to pick up the slack in his work.

Pete could have attacked Kathryn personally by calling her a slob and then accuse her of creating a pigsty that both of them are forced to work in. Pete probably would get nowhere and Kathryn would become hostile. By helping Pete to formulate his confrontation plan, you're helping him to resolve the conflict between him and Kathryn.

WYIFB is a great tool that can be used in many situations. It's impossible for someone to dispute how you feel. When you help your employees to develop these skills, you've giving them permission to act as adults and handle coworker-to-coworker conflict independently without your intervention.

There are times, however, when conflicts can't be resolved and they evolve into complaints. Once this happens, you'll have to conduct an investigation in order to find the truth.

Chapter 11

Dotting Your I's

As in Investigation. As a manager, you may find yourself in a position to conduct an investigation, particularly if you work for a small company that does not have a human resources function in place. Don't let the term "investigation" intimidate you. It's just a process you need to follow in order to find the truth. That's it. Investigations must occur when there are two opposing viewpoints and a resolution has not been reached.

It's important that you know how to conduct an investigation. Once you understand how an investigation is conducted, you'll be able to follow the steps and conduct one of your own.

We'll start with something simple. Like harassment.

Harry and his supervisor don't get along. As their manager, you've sensed that for some time but you were hoping they'd get over it. Finally, one day, Harry can't take it anymore and files a formal complaint against Frieda.

"She's harassing me. She's on me from the minute I get in until I clock out. She treats me differently from everyone else and I'm tired of it. I'm the only one in the entire department who has to live up to her impossible standards."

"Harry, exactly what is your complaint? You need to be specific."

"Frieda is harassing me. "

"Give me specific examples of her behavior that you consider harassing.

"She yells at me. She's accused me of doing things wrong. And I can tell that she doesn't like me. She just treats me differently."

"Well, Harry, if you believe Frieda is harassing you, then I need to investigate it. I'll need to talk to at least Frieda. Do you work with anyone who has witnessed Frieda harassing you?"

"Yes. Sam, Miranda, and Penelope. They've all witnessed it. And I think Miranda will say that Frieda harasses her too. Go ahead and call them. They'll back me up."

"What about Susan? Shouldn't I call Susan too? And I will need to speak with Frieda as well."

"Fine. Talk to Susan but she's a suck up so everything Frieda does is fine with her. But call her anyway. I don't care."

"Harry, I'll call Frieda first. I'll need to tell her that you've filed a formal complaint of harassment."

"Hey, what if it gets worse. I don't need that!"

"I'll also explain to Frieda that she's not to treat you any differently because of the complaint. Or I could transfer you to another department, temporarily, until the investigation is complete."

"Yes, transfer me. I simply cannot work for Frieda. She's a tyrant and a harasser and I won't be subjected to that treatment any longer. I do like my job and I like everyone I work with. Except Frieda. She's out to get me. Wait till you talk to her. You'll get it."

"Okay. I'll make arrangements to move you temporarily to Shipping. It's a much different job than you're currently doing, but, for now, it makes sense to get you out of that department. I'll need to speak with everyone you've given me permission to speak with and explain that you've filed this complaint. And then I'll ask each of them some questions. Once I've interviewed everyone, I'll schedule a meeting with you to let you know what I've found out."

Your first call should be to Frieda. It can go like this, "Frieda, this is Deb Whitworth in HR. I've just met with Harry from your department and he's filed a complaint of harassment against you. I'll be investigating his claim and I'd like to meet with you first. Could we meet this afternoon in my office?" She may be surprised and she'll agree to meet. You can end the conversation by saying something like, "Frieda, I don't need to remind you that any behavior that could be termed "retaliatory" is forbidden."

At this point, you need to schedule interviews with each individual. Explain briefly why you need to speak with everyone and try to do this as quickly as possible. You can say something like this, "Hi, Sam. This is Deb Whitworth is HR. Harry Turner and I have met today and he has filed a complaint of harassment against Frieda. I'm conducting an investigation and would like to meet with you this afternoon if possible. It's important that the nature of this conversation and our meeting remain between us so I'm asking you not to speak with your coworkers about this." You can't guarantee confidentiality, but it is your responsibility to maintain it to the best of your ability.

You need to ask each individual the same questions, although your questions to the accused party will be a bit different. Have your questions prepared in advance on a legal pad with space provided between each one so that you can write the answers. In this particular situation, you could ask questions along the following lines:

1.   Start the meeting by stating the nature of the complaint: "As I mentioned over the phone, Harry has filed a complaint of harassment against Frieda. I hope you haven't talked to anyone about this. It's important that we maintain, to the best of our ability, both Harry's and Frieda's confidentiality. Certainly, you can imagine what it would be like to be either Harry or Frieda and I'm sure you'd like your own confidentiality protected."

2.   "Could you explain to me what you believe harassment is?"

3.   "Can you give me an example of a time when you've witnessed Frieda harassing Harry?"

4.   Can you think of any other examples of times when you've witnessed Frieda harassing Harry?"

5.   "Have you ever witnessed Frieda harassing anyone else in the department?"

6.   "Has Frieda ever harassed you?"

You have asked for no opinions. You've asked for facts and your decision will be based on the facts you've received. The evidence may be overwhelming in one direction or another. It could also be a draw.

If the evidence shows that Frieda is guilty of harassment, then you would follow your disciplinary policy, which should provide progressive disciplinary. In this case, Frieda would be given a disciplinary warning. Even if this is Frieda's first offense and your policy calls for a verbal warning, it's serious enough that it warrants a written warning with a copy of it placed in her personnel file.

Harassment must be taken very seriously. Frieda will also be told that any behavior that could be deemed as retaliatory in nature will not be tolerated and will result in termination of employment. During your follow up meeting with Harry you will explain your findings and let him know that appropriate disciplinary action has been taken. He may want to see Frieda get fired. That is not his decision to make. You can assure him that appropriate action has been taken and that retaliatory behavior will not be tolerated. He can resume his duties in the department. If there is another position open in another department that he'd like to apply for, that is an option. You don't have to create a position for him but you must be able to assure him that the harassing behavior will stop and then you must ensure that it does. If the harassment continues or if retaliatory measures are taken by Frieda, employment termination would result, as you've told her in your meeting which you have followed up in a memo to her with a copy to her personnel file.

If the evidence shows that Frieda is not guilty of harassment, Harry must be told that you could find no evidence of harassment during your interviews with the employees that he wanted you to speak with. You should speak with Harry personally, either by phone or in person if practical, and then follow up your conversation with a letter sent certified mail, return receipt requested.

Harry probably won't like your conclusion if you've found that harassment has not taken place. You should then direct him to the next step in your internal complaint procedure which is typically the next step in the chain of command. That could be the president of the company or the person to whom you report. That individual will review your investigation notes and may or may not conduct an investigation of his/her own. This should be spelled out in your internal complaint procedure. And you should also direct Harry to your state's human rights commission. He can always file an external complaint.

Should Harry choose to file an external complaint, your documentation will be extremely valuable. Take good notes, date them, and put them in a file labeled "Investigation Notes."

If your company does not have an internal complaint procedure, it should. You should have something like the following in place in order to give employees a vehicle for filing an internal complaint. You'd much rather an internal complaint be filed than an external one to the human rights commission, so give them a way to do that. Of course, an external complaint can be filed in lieu of an internal complaint. But when you provide that mechanism, the chances are good that it will be used. And when it's used, it gives you an opportunity to conduct an investigation and find the truth.

Internal Complaint Procedure

It is the policy of Zortron to provide an appropriate vehicle for employees to seek review of problems related to working conditions, supervision, co-workers, and other work-related matters that have not been resolved in an informal manner.

Procedure

1. **The employee should seek a resolution to the work-related problem with the employee's immediate supervisor or manager.**

2. **If the employee is dissatisfied, the concern should be presented in writing to the employee's immediate supervisor or manager within 10 days of the event or within seven days if related to employment separation. The supervisor/manager will respond in writing within seven days of receipt of document. (If the employee prefers, s/he can instead go directly to the TITLE OF HR REPRESENTATIVE within the same timeframe.)**

3.   Within seven days of the supervisor's or manager's written response to the employee, the employee may appeal, in writing, the finding of the supervisor or manager to the TITLE OF HR REPRESENTATIVE. The TITLE OF HR REPRESENTATIVE will investigate the facts and present a response in writing within seven days of receipt.

4.   The decision of the HR REPRESENTATIVE may be appealed within seven days to the President or CEO. After reviewing all information, the President or CEO will render a final decision within 10 days. The employee will be informed verbally and in writing, and all personnel involved in the process will be informed.

5.   The concerned employee may be accompanied by a fellow employee at any step of this process.

6.   If you feel your complaint has not been appropriately handled by Zortron, you may call the STATE Human Rights Commission at PHONE NUMBER.

Again, Harry may not feel comfortable returning to his former department. You would offer him the same option as you would had the decision gone in his favor. You don't have to create a position for him but you should help him find another position in another department if that is his preference. He'll have to decide whether or not he wants to remain employed with the company. It's up to you to assure him that retaliatory behavior will not be tolerated, either by the manager or by him.

Chapter 12

The End is Here

Sometimes, no matter how hard you try, no matter how good a supervisor you are, and no matter how tolerant you are, an employee just isn't going to make it. You need to know the signs that point to The End of the Employment Life Cycle and then help your employee to exit with dignity, regardless of the reason for employment termination.

It does you and your company no good "to have the last word" or "to get even" or "to show the employee who's boss after all." The manner in which you allow an employee to exit your company could one day mean the difference between winning a discrimination claim, a lawsuit, or re-employment rights.

Let's talk about how an employee gets to the end of his/her employment life cycle. There are a lot of reasons, among them the employee has

> Outgrown the job
> Not learned the job
> Grown bored
> Found it necessary to move on due to family circumstances
> Found a job in his/her field of study
> Breached company policy

Whatever the reason, it comes down to either a voluntary or involuntary separation of employment. In other words, the employee is leaving on his/her own or you're terminating the employment relationship with that individual.

When an employee has outgrown the job, there could be other company opportunities s/he wants to pursue. This can easily be handled through your company's internal job posting program. Although it's difficult, at times, for managers to accept an employee's decision to pursue other company interests, and, consequently, be forced to train a replacement, it's never fair to hold an employee back for your own selfishness. Encourage your employees to look for internal opportunities. Your department's loss could be the company's gain. And if the employee has outgrown the job, s/he'll look elsewhere if nothing is available internally.

It may happen that an employee does not learn the job s/he was hired to fill. If you're comfortable that you've provided adequate training, your judgment may be that the employee simply isn't going to learn the job. Or the employee could have exaggerated his/her past experience on the job application and during the interview. If you determine this to be the case, don't prolong your decision. It's best to admit your mistake—the interview either was not thorough enough or the employee is a good liar. In either case, it's best to allow the employee to move on to something s/he is more suited for.

Sometimes employees grow bored with their jobs. Let's face it, many jobs are simply what they are and there is no way to make them more challenging, more

Chapter 13
The End is Here

stimulating, or more interesting. I've known employees in what I would call boring jobs to remain content for years. They come in, do the rather mindless work, and go home. They're getting what they want from the job—the satisfaction of doing it well and being compensated fairly for it. Again, if your company posts positions internally, an employee who likes working for your company will pursue other positions within the company. However, some employees will simply choose to go in another direction.

There are times when a spouse of an employee will accept employment in another geographic area. There's little you can do to keep an employee back under these circumstances. And if an employee has been working his/her way through college, you must also accept the fact that upon graduation, s/he will look for a position in his/her own field of study.

And then you'll have a situation when an employee breaches company policy. When this is the case, or you suspect that this is the case, it's important that you not let emotion take control and "fire on the spot." I can't think of any reason whatsoever when it would be appropriate to fire someone on the spot. INVESTIGATE. Even if you see Bill slug Sam, don't fire Bill on the spot. He may simply have been defending himself!

How do you fire someone? Let me say first that firing someone is a life-changing event-- and not just for the person being fired. It should be a life-changing event for the person responsible for the firing as well. Don't ever fire someone you're not convinced deserves to be fired. And even when that person deserves it and it's the right thing to do, the act of firing him/her should change your life in some way. You're dealing with a human being, after all. And after 20 years and countless employment terminations, I still don't sleep the night before, I still get nauseous, and I perspire more than I have a right to. And this is all good.

When, fairly new to the job almost 20 years ago, I was faced with terminating the employment of an employee who clearly needed to be fired. I was, nonetheless, a bit nervous. She had stolen stamp money. There was no doubt about it, and the investigation was completed by my boss. The employee to be fired was quite a bit bigger than me and I think deep down I thought she might hurt me. My supervisor at the time, the Executive Director of this nonprofit organization, told me not to worry. . ."the more often you fire people, the easier it will get." I told him, "I hope not." Because the day it becomes easy, the day it's just another task on my to-do list, the day I feel rested from a good night's sleep prior to an employment termination. . .well, that's the day I should get out of human resources and open a craft store.

So, you've decided that employment termination is the next step in Bob's employment life cycle. What's the process you follow to actually fire Bob? It should come directly from your progressive disciplinary policy. And it should include a phrase that allows a manager to terminate employment without following those steps when the safety of an employee, vendor, or customer is threatened by the employee's continued employment. But this does not excuse you from conducting an investigation. Sometimes that investigation may simply be a meeting with an employee and noting in a follow-up memo the behavior that must be changed. You don't need to speak with other employees, only to the employee who is not following company policy or procedure.

Always fire an employee for one reason. Even if you've finally reached your limit with tolerating inappropriate workplace behavior, you need to know exactly why you've decided to terminate employment.

For instance, let's consider Bob again. He's the employee who consistently shows up late to work. You've decided to fire him today. You've had it. You're done paying him for time that he has not worked. In your view, Bob is stealing from the company. Okay, so what is the deciding factor? If you have allowed him to be late for six weeks and have not spoken to him about it, then what makes today different from any of those other days? Why, all of a sudden do you decide to no longer tolerate his lateness? The fact that you haven't said anything to Bob allows him to assume that it's okay to be late, otherwise "my supervisor would have said something."

Why fire Bob today? Answer is: Don't do it. It's not fair. You haven't been honest with Bob about your expectations. You've led him to believe that late is okay. Instead, give him fair warning by meeting with him and then following up your meeting in a memo with a copy for the personnel file. "You've been late off and on for six weeks and I've tolerated it thinking that you would correct this on your own. Obviously you are not going to do that. You have one week to make arrangements to arrive on time each and every day. If you are late again after

(DATE one week from memo date) your employment will be terminated. Consider this notice to that effect."

It may sound too generous to give an employee a week to arrange to be to work on time. After all, that IS the expectation. But remember, you've allowed this to go on for six weeks. So, really, it's NOT the expectation. Maybe Bob has transportation issues, childcare issues, or other personal reasons. By giving him fair warning, you're giving him one last chance and giving him the opportunity to succeed. Think about it--by allowing the behavior to continue, you've actually altered job expectations. I don't think it's stretching things to say you're to blame for this, not Bob.

Always terminate employment with dignity. Do it privately but with another person present, preferably another manager, your HR manager, or another person in a supervisory capacity. Why? To serve as a witness should the employee make accusations about you or the process in the future. Here are some steps to follow:

1.   Investigate and determine the reason for the termination of employment.

2.   Be able to state in one sentence the reason for the termination.

3.   Decide if termination is the best course of action—if you aren't comfortable with 1 and 2, then decide what your alternative strategy will be.

4.   Provide a memo to the employee documenting the reason for the termination; allow a space for employee comments and employee signature .

5.   Make arrangements to meet with the employee privately, but with another manager present as witness; this should be at a time that allows the employee to exit with dignity (break time, after work, when the work area is sparsely populated).

6.   Invite the employee to sit down.

7.   Tell the employee that because of REASON, his/her employment is terminated, effective immediately.

8.   Have the employee read the memo and invite him/her to ask questions, make comments, and sign the memo.

9.   An angry employee may refuse to provide comments and/or sign the memo; the other manager will sign as witness noting that the employee refused to sign (An angry employee may refuse to read beyond the first line).

10.   Offer the employee a copy of the signed memo.

11.   Escort the employee to his/her work area and allow him/her to get personal belongings.

12.   Collect keys, company property, employee handbook, etc.

13.   Escort the employee to the door.

14.   Immediately notify your technology department (if applicable) of the termination.

15.   Be prepared to answer questions from other employees without breaching the exiting employee's confidentiality.

16.   Announce to those who have a need to know that this employee is no longer employed by your company, effective today; you need not provide details.

17.   Send the former employee an Exit Interview Questionnaire.

What happens if, during your meeting, the employee brings up information that you didn't have, that would change your mind about the termination? First of all, if this happens, you did not investigate thoroughly. Shame on you. And you call yourself a manager. This should NEVER happen. However, if it does happen, you are, in effect, firing on the spot because you don't have all the information you need to make an informed decision. An investigation means that you know everything you can possibly know about the situation in order to make an appropriate decision.

Okay, so what if that *does* happen. The employee who you are firing turns the tables and says something that floors you--that causes you to change your mind.

DON'T continue with the termination. If you find out something that you may have had no way of knowing and this information does change your mind, then allow your mind to change. Don't make the situation worse than it already is. Tell the employee that s/he is giving you new information that you'll have to investigate. Ask him/her how you can confirm the information. Turn this meeting into a fact-finding meeting, rather than an employment termination meeting. Then schedule a subsequent meeting. This new information may be confirmed, in which case you apologize and learn a lesson in conducting investigations so this doesn't happen again. Or this information may not be confirmed, in which case your decision to terminate employment stands.

Don't discount the information as invalid without investigating. That's very risky. At most, employment may be prolonged several days. Or it may not be prolonged beyond the end of the day. But take the employee's words seriously. Based on the circumstances, you may want to send the employee home with pay until you can confirm or not confirm the information. Again, a small price to pay in order to avoid future risk.

Now let's look at another situation. What happens if, during the meeting, the employee becomes irate, swears at you and calls you names. If this hasn't happened to you, be forewarned—it will. How should you handle it? First of all, keep your distance. If appropriate, call security or call the front desk and ask them to call security or the police if the situation is really out of hand.

I had this happen once. As the HR vice president, I conducted the termination meeting between the manager and the soon-to-be exiting employee. This employee became irate and slammed my door open, left my office and yelled obscenities as he stormed down the hall, tossing cell phone, keys, and pager behind him. I think he was hoping to hit me. His manager and I followed him, at a safe distance, down the hall and watched as he emptied his desk. He was not worried about protecting his dignity or confidentiality and we never had the opportunity to make that offer to him. He left in a fury.

We didn't have the chance to offer him a copy of his termination memo because he lost his temper. He never signed the memo, so his manager signed it as witness. But the story isn't over. He called and left a message on my voice mail several weeks later requesting a copy of the memo. Was I obligated to provide it? Yes. I sent him a copy, certified mail, return receipt requested. His actions, no matter how irresponsible, did not absolve me from my responsibility.

Let's discuss each step in the employment termination process.

Investigate the reason for the termination of employment
You may think that investigation isn't important if a complaint has not been made. But think about it. In every situation, there IS a complaint. It may not be a complaint of harassment, for instance, that you'd know to investigate. But any employment termination is based on a complaint. What is it if the employee just isn't working out? A complaint maybe that this employee isn't meeting the job expectations. What is it if the employee doesn't want to work for your company

any longer? A complaint that maybe the job isn't living up to his/her expectations. What is it if the employee has breached company policy or has inappropriately shared proprietary information. A complaint that the employee acted inappropriately and possibly put the company at risk. In each and every instance, the reason comes down to a complaint of some sort. We investigate complaints, we take complaints seriously, we act on complaints.

Be able to state in one sentence the reason for the termination
You need to be able to state very clearly why termination is the next step in this employee's employment life cycle. If you can't get the reason down to one sentence, you haven't thought enough about the reason for the termination. Whether the employee is late almost ever day, treats other employees with disrespect, isn't performing the job satisfactorily, or can't get along with his/her supervisor, there is a reason there.

Decide if termination is the best course of action
Under certain circumstances you can definitely consider alternatives to ending the employment relationship. Obviously, if you are terminating employment due to a breach of a company policy, for instance, that is the only option (after you've completed your investigation). If there is a personality conflict between the employee and another employee, maybe a transfer is in order. If the employee is late all of the time, maybe it's because the schedule no longer works, but the employee is someone you'd like to keep. Then consider other schedules or other departments where the schedule does fit. Look at all of your options before letting a good employee go.

Document the reason for the termination

If you are terminating employment, then upon request, an employee is entitled to a written reason for his/her termination of employment. Have it ready and then offer a copy to the employee. Allow a space for the employee to make comments ("they never even listened to MY side of things") and sign. There is nothing to be gained by not allowing an employee to vent before exiting.

Meet privately

Always allow an exiting employee to exit with dignity. This means that you may have to meet at a time that isn't convenient for you. But this meeting isn't about you--it's about the exiting employee. It works well to meet during other employees' break time, before or after work, or at another time when the work area is quiet so that personal belongings can be retrieved. When it isn't practical to schedule a meeting for one of these times, offer to have the employee come back after work when everyone, except another manager, has gone home for the day. There is no need and nothing to be gained from using an exiting employee as an example. Your goal is to end the employment relationship, nothing more. Share information with other managers regarding the termination on a need-to-know basis only.

Invite the employee to sit down

Most times, an exiting employee knows why you're meeting before you even open your mouth. An employee should not be surprised, even though s/he may act surprised. If you have followed your disciplinary procedures, this employee will know what the next step is because you've given fair warning. S/he will be nervous. Under the circumstances, this will be a difficult meeting, but try to make it as dignified as possible.

State the reason for the meeting

Don't keep the employee guessing why this meeting is being called to order. Don't apologize, don't get emotional, state the facts. "Sharon, we're meeting today because we've decided to terminate your employment with COMPANY, effective immediately. I've prepared this memo that should explain everything. Please take the next few minutes to read it."

Allow employee time to read the memo

Once the employee has read the memo, ask if there are any questions. Invite the employee to provide comments in the section provided and then ask him/her to sign the memo. When this doesn't happen, explain that signing the memo does not indicate agreement, simply that the memo was read and received. If the employee still refuses to sign it, ask the attending witness to sign in the employee's place noting that "employee refused to sign memo."

Offer a copy of the memo

Once the comments and signature are in place, offer the employee a copy. Ask the attending manager to make the copy. It's not a good idea to leave the employee unattended in your office. If you meet in the other manager's office, you should offer to make the copy.

Escort the employee to his/her work area

At this point, you shouldn't allow the employee unrestricted access to anywhere in the building. Should something "questionable" occur, s/he could be unreasonably blamed for it. Or s/he could actually be responsible for it. Neither situation is good, which is why I strongly encourage an escort, even when you "know s/he'd never do anything." You should have arranged to have the meeting take place during break time or, when that's not possible, suggest the employee come back to the work place after work to retrieve personal belongings. The employee may just want to get it over with, but it's important that you have made the offer. While the employee is getting personal belongings (have a box ready), make sure you collect keys and other company property and that the employee doesn't take what doesn't belong to him/her. This is less likely to occur when you're watching the employee fill the box with personal items.

Escort the employee to the door

Again, do not allow the employee unrestricted access to the building.

Immediately notify technology department

It's important that the employment termination triggers the termination of voice mail, email, and other technology that requires a password or is proprietary in nature. Voice mail messages can be sent to the supervisor's mailbox; likewise with email messages.

Be prepared for questions

Know exactly what you will say to other employees and managers who ask "why." You may not breach the exiting employee's confidentiality, nor may you share information with those who do not have a need to know.

Announce the departure

When you announce that Sharon is no longer employed by your company, your statement could go something like this, "Sharon no longer works for COMPANY, effective immediately." If you're questioned further you can reply, "If you need further information, you should speak personally with Sharon." If the person asking the question is not a personal friend of Sharon's, s/he probably won't know how to reach her and, therefore, has no need to know. You don't owe anyone an explanation beyond those who have a need to know (upper management, for instance).

Conclusion

So, now you know everything I know. Management is not difficult, like most things, if you have the passion to learn it and the toolbox with the right tools tucked inside. There are those who would have you believe that it's "hard" but only because they want to make it look like they work "hard" at it. But it's not. And I've shown you that. Look around. The best managers I know are those who make it look easy. In fact, the best people at anything make it look easy.

Be a role model.

Follow the process.

Treat people fairly.

PRODUCTIVE PUBLICATIONS

Books to Help You Succeed

CATALOGUE

For more detailed information visit us on the Internet

Canadian Web Site:
http://www.productivepublications.ca
**or call 1-(800) 829-1317 (24 hrs) for a free
printed copy of our latest Canadian catalogue**

American Web Site:
http://www.productivepublications.com
**or call 1-(800) 850-4636 (24 hrs) for a free
printed copy of our latest American catalogue**

Serving Readers for Over 18 years

"You're Hired....
You're Fired!"

**A Manager's Guide to
Employee Supervision**

By: Deborah L. Whitworth

This book is a great read if you are a manager or a supervisor; even if it is only being in charge temporarily for a day. It will provide you with a step-by-step method of acquiring practical human resource management skills.

Author, Deborah L. Whitworth, has been a human resource manager for over 20 years. She believes that management isn't rocket science but a process. You want to do the right thing. Unfortunately, nobody has told you what the right thing is. Deborah acts as a role model and shows you how to manage yourself, so you can be free to manager others.

144 pages, ISBN 1-55270-146-8 Softcover: Canadian: $24.95; USA $19.95; UK: £12.48

MAKE IT! MARKET IT! BANK IT!

Over 100 Ways to Start Your Own Home-Based Business

By: Barbara J. Albrecht

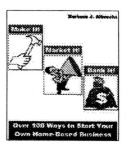

This book is about starting your own home-based business. It's also about earning extra money when your wages don't stretch far enough. Money for vacations and education often fall through the cracks in your financial plans and you may find that you need a second income.

Newspaper columnist, Barb Albrecht, has assembled these100 great ideas to help you put cash into your "money jar". If you're looking to run your own part-time business or start a new career as owner of your own enterprise....you owe it to yourself to read this book.

144 pages, ISBN 1-55270-145-X softcover: Canada: $24.95 USA $19.95 UK: £12.48

Make Money Trading in Options

How to Start Immediately

By: Jason Diptee

Want to invest in an expensive stock, the Japanese Yen or the DOW but only have $200- $300 to invest? Option trading allows you to enter these markets to take advantage of investment opportunities that would otherwise require thousands of dollars. This book will teach beginners how to participate in the largely untapped and unknown area of investing that can generate profits in a matter of weeks.

Jason Diptee holds an MBA and is an experienced seminar leader on the subject of option trading.

116 pages, ISBN 1-55270-150-6 Softcover: Canadian $24.95; USA: $19.95; UK: £12.48

Welcome to the Business World:

April 2004A Guide to Help You Get Started in Your New Job

By: V. Harvey Mortensen

You've recently graduated and you've just landed a job. Alternatively, you may have switched jobs and joined a new company. What does that really mean? What is expected of you? How will you fit in? How will you advance in the business?

V. Harvey Mortensen helps you answer these questions so that you can embark on a rewarding career in the business world. He shows you how to become a valuable "asset" for the company you work for. He also demonstrates how to plan and get organized and then to set objectives for yourself.

182 pages, ISBN 1-55270-147-6 Softcover: Canada: $26.95; USA: $21.95; UK: £13.48

**You can obtain further information online at:
Canadian Web site: *http://www.productivepublications.ca*
American Web site: *http://www.productivepublications.com*
Order online or complete the order form at the end of this catalogue**

**Business Planning
and Finances**

**Confederation College
Entrepreneurship Series**

**Business Relationships –
Development and
Maintenance**

**Confederation College
Entrepreneurship Series**

Business Planning and Finances takes a pragmatic and hands-on approach to business planning and financial management, and is written in straightforward language free of technical jargon. It includes a thorough review of the role of planning, the benefits to be realized from planning, and the use of a plan as a management aid.

Business Planning and Finances Confederation College Entrepreneurship Series, 174 pages, ISBN: 1-55270-091-7 Softcover   Canada: $34.95   USA: $25.95   UK: £17.48

The success of any business hinges on the effective management of three critical categories of business relationships. These are a firm's relationships with its customers, with its employees, and with the individuals and organizations that supply it with essential goods and services.

Business Relationships – Development and Maintenance Confederation College Entrepreneurship Series, 78 pages, ISBN: 1-55270-093-3, Softcover
Canada: $19.95   USA: $14.95   UK: £9.98

*Modern Materials
Management Techniques:
A Complete Guide to Help
You Plan, Direct and Control
the Purchase, Production,
Storage and Distribution of
Goods in Today's
Competitive Business
Environment–Essentials of
Supply Chain Management*

By: Paula Mackie

Covers the entire process of a company's operations relating to the acquisition of goods and services. Written for both the public and private sectors as well as college and university educators.

Modern Materials Management Techniques: 390 pages, softcover, ISBN: 1-55270-121-2   Canada: $94.95 USA: $69.95   UK: £47.48

**Software for Small
Business
2001 Edition**

**A review of the latest
Windows programs to
help you improve
business
efficiency and productivity**

By: Iain Williamson

For new and experienced users. Covers operating systems, word processing, desktop publishing, voice dictation, graphics, video, photos, spreadsheets, accounting, databases, contact management, communications, Internet software, security and virus protection.

Software for Small Business: 2001 Edition: by Iain Williamson: 345 pages, softcover; ISBN 1-55270-082-8 Canada: $39.95   USA: $29.95   UK: £19.98

**You can obtain further information online at:
Canadian Web site: *http://www.productivepublications.ca*
American Web site: *http://www.productivepublications.com*
Order online or complete the order form at the end of this catalogue**

Web Marketing for Small & Home-Based Businesses:

How to Advertise and Sell Your Products Online

By: Learn2succed.com Incorporated

This book shows you how to advertise and sell your products or services on the Web. Learn the basics of e-commerce and some of the challenges facing online merchants. Find out about search engines and how to improve your listings with them. Keep you name in front of your customers with permission-based e-mail and electronic newsletters. Don't forget the importance of referrals. How to use traditional marketing to drive traffic to your site. Find out about the importance of web links and associate programs.

132 pages, ISBN 1-55270-119-0 softcover: Canada: $24.95; USA: $19.95; UK: £12.48

Inexpensive E-Commerce Solutions for Small & Home-Based Businesses:

You Don't Have to Spend a Fortune to Start Selling Online

By: Learn2succed.com Incorporated

How to sell your products or services on the Web without spending a fortune. Learn the secrets of selecting a suitable domain name. How to accept payment and how to deal with international currencies. The fulfilment process and why timely delivery is so important. Why security and privacy are such important issues for your customers and how to address them.

Take a quick tour of inexpensive e-commerce software that do not require any programming knowledge and can get you up and running in no time.

130 pages, ISBN 1-55270-118-2 softcover: Canada: $24.95; USA: $19.95 UK: £12.48

Harness the POWER of the Internet:

Easy Ways to Put Your Business on the World Wide Web

By: Michael L. Williams

Step-by-step methods to market your business, promote your wares; make a fortune....or just have a great time utilizing the Internet to its fullest advantage....this very comprehensive book shows you how to do it without any programming knowledge.

Michael L. Williams has developed and marketed educational and software programs for pre-school and grade school children. He has been Internet consultant and is now a software quality assurance engineer.

216 pages, ISBN 1-55270-142-5 Softcover Canada: $39.95; USA: $29.95; UK: £19.98

How to Get Started with Little or No Programming Knowledge

By: Michael L. Williams

This very comprehensive book covers all the essentials you need to know: domain names, web hosting, web design, Form Mail, search engines, portals and browsers. How to advertise and promote your client's business; how to fine-tune the site and find out who visits and what they look at. Learn how to become indispensable and keep your client. Find out about legal matters, tech support, maintenance fees, quality assurance, security, viruses and hackers.

Michael L. Williams has experience as a software developer and marketer, as an Internet consultant and he is now a software quality assurance engineer.

260 pages, ISBN 1-55270-143-3 Softcover: Canada: $39.95; USA: $29.95; UK: £19.98

You can obtain further information online at:
Canadian Web site: *http://www.productivepublications.ca*
American Web site: *http://www.productivepublications.com*
Order online or complete the order form at the end of this catalogue

Your Guide to Financing Business Growth by Selling a Piece of the Pie

What's involved in going public; employee share ownership plans and franchising in Canada

Revised and Updated 2003-2004 Edition

By: Iain Williamson

A critical examination of three methods of growing your business by using other people's money. How to sell shares to the public or to your employees. How to expand through franchising. The author was a financial analyst in the Canadian stockbrokerage business.

108 pages; Softcover; ISBN 1-55270-126-3; ISSN 1191-0488: Canada: $21.95

Your Guide to Canadian Export Financing: Successful Techniques for Financing Your Exports from Canada

Revised 2003-2004 Edition

By: Iain Williamson

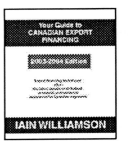

Practical techniques for financing exports. Get details of all provincial and federal assistance programs that help you export including addresses and phone numbers to steer you in the right direction. The author is a consultant and entrepreneur who knows the practical side of importing and exporting.

Iain Williamson is an entrepreneur, business consultant and seminar leader. He has considerable experience in import-export.

174 pages; softcover; ISBN 1-55270-127-1; ISSN: 1191-047X Canada: $32.95

Your Guide to Government Financial Assistance for Business

(Separate Editions-one for each Province & Territory)

Revised 2003-2004 Editions

By: Iain Williamson

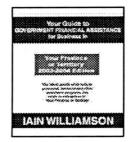

Business financing in Canada is in a constant state of flux. New government programs are continually being introduced. Old ones are often amended or discontinued with little publicity. These books will provide you with the latest information on all Federal and Provincial/Territorial programs that specifically relate to each area.

Author, Iain Williamson, of Entrepreneurial Business Consultants of Canada, has over 30 years experience as a stock market financial analyst and as owner-manager of his own companies.

Softcover: each cost $44.95
Title & ISBN List appears on right ➜

Your Guide to Government Financial Assistance for Business In...

EDITION	ISBN	PAGES
Newfoundland & Labrador	155270128X	344
Prince Edward Island	1552701298	318
Nova Scotia	1552701301	304
New Brunswick	155270131X	298
Quebec	1552701328	348
Ontario	1552701336	344
Manitoba	1552701344	354
Saskatchewan	1552701352	338
Alberta	1552701360	330
British Columbia	1552701379	344
The Yukon	1552701387	266
The Northwest Territories	1552701395	280
The Nunavut	1552701409	270

Please specify Province or Territory when ordering. All titles are $44.95 ea.

You can obtain further information online at:
Canadian Web site: *http://www.productivepublications.ca*
American Web site: *http://www.productivepublications.com*
Order online or complete the order form at the end of this catalogue

Your Guide to Starting & Self-Financing Your Own Business in Canada

Revised 2003-2004 Edition

By: Iain Williamson

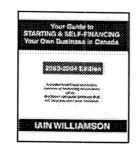

This 2003/2004 Edition has been updated and revised to reflect the many changes that have taken place in the sources of marketing information and a chapter has been added on getting marketing information from the Internet. There is a chapter on the use of computers and how they can help you run your business more efficiently and save money and time.

222 pages; Softcover; ISBN 1-55270-122-0; ISSN 1191-0518 Canada: $24.95

Your Guide to Preparing a Plan to Raise Money for Your Own Business

Revised 2003-2004 Edition

By: Iain Williamson

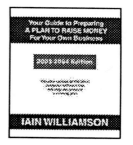

A good business plan is essential to succeed in your quest for financing. Contains a step-by-step guide to create your own winning plan. Computer software you can use. Learn how to address the concerns of investors or lenders. Tips on structuring your plan. Contains a sample plan to show you an example

The author is a consultant with many years of experience in preparing plans for business clients.

172 pages, softcover, ISBN 1-55270-123-9; ISSN 1191-0496 Canada: $24.95

Your Guide to Raising Venture Capital for Your Own Business in Canada

Revised and Updated 2003-2004 Edition

By: Iain Williamson

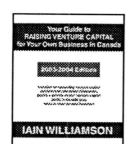

This book is a gold mine of information for anyone who is raising venture capital in Canada. It shows you how to do it yourself. It discusses the structure of the industry; what venture capitalists are looking for and how they evaluate deals. It tells you how to contact them. Find out what informal investors or "angels" can offer and how to find them. You can see if corporate angels and intermediaries can be of assistance.

244 pages, Softcover; ISBN 1-55270-124-7; ISSN 1191-0534 Canada: $36.95

Your Guide to Arranging Bank & Debt Financing for Your Own Business in Canada

Revised and Updated 2003-2004 Edition

By: Iain Williamson

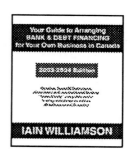

Learn the secrets of successful debt financing in Canada. Find out who the players are in Canadian banking. Do you qualify for the new high risk, unsecured loans? How to prepare your company before you approach lenders. Find out how your loan application is evaluated. Can factoring or leasing help you? The author has many years of experience in bank financing and leasing.

230 pages; Softcover; ISBN 1-55270-125-5; ISSN 1191-0542 Canada: $32.95

You can obtain further information online at:
Canadian Web site: *http://www.productivepublications.ca*
American Web site: *http://www.productivepublications.com*
Order online or complete the order form at the end of this catalogue

Short Cut to Easy Street

How to Get Money in Your Mailbox Every Day, Plus Automatic Income for the Rest of Your Life

By: Stephen W. Kenyon

A great book on self-motivation, direct mail, self-publishing, marketing/advertising/promoting and network marketing. Study and learn the details of Stephen Kenyon's fascinating system for attracting wealth and success.

Author, **Stephen Kenyon**, shares with you the inside trade secrets and techniques which he learned over a 30-year period.

244 pages, Softcover; ISBN 1-55270-057-7 Canada: $37.95
USA: $27.95   UK: £18.98

Start Your Own Business: Be Your Own Boss!

Your Road Map to Independence

By: Iain Williamson

Learn from someone who has done it! What it takes! Where to get ideas and how to check them out. How to research the market. Calculate how much money you will really need and where to get it. Growing pains and managing employees... plus lots more.

Iain Williamson has run his own businesses for over 24 years and is a consultant. He'll help you with a Road Map to Independence!

208 pages; Softcover; ISBN 1-896210-96-1:   Canada: $29.95
USA: $21.95   UK: £14.98

Becoming Successful!

Taking Your Home-Based Business to a New Level

By: Don Varner

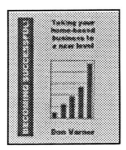

Strategies for getting great results in your home-based business! How to turn any type of business into a SUCCESSFUL business!

- Self-Improvement
- Handling Rejections
- Management Skills
- 16 Ways to Prospect
- Designing Great Ads
- Self-Motivation
- Hiring Tips
- Motivating Employees
- Closing Sales
- No-Cost Ways to Advertise

338 pgs; ISBN 1-896210-87-2; Softcover   Canada: $39.95
USA: $29.95   UK: £19.98

Timeless Strategies to Become a Successful Entrepreneur

By: Lawrence Scott Troemel

Strategies for starting, building, and managing a small business. These approaches have been successfully implemented for decades and will continue to be viable well into the future. Every entrepreneur will benefit from the advice in this very readable book that is full of interesting anecdotes.

208 pages; ISBN 1-55270-046-1; softcover: Canada: $29.95
USA: $21.95   UK: £14.98

You can obtain further information online at:
Canadian Web site: *http://www.productivepublications.ca*
American Web site: *http://www.productivepublications.com*
Order online or complete the order form at the end of this catalogue

Savvy Women Entrepreneurs

Twenty-Eight Different Women Share the Secrets To Their Business Success

By: Kristina Liehr

Can You Make Money with Your Idea or Invention?

By: Don Lunny

You don't have to go to business school to start a business! Learn how 28 remarkable women entrepreneurs started their own business; many in their garage or kitchen. Read about the steps that they took; the obstacles they overcame and the joy, happiness and success that they achieved. The chances they took and how they learned from their mistakes. Get the confidence and inspiration to start YOUR own business or EARN EXTRA INCOME.

140 pages; Softcover; ISBN 1-55270-000-3 Canada: $24.95
USA: $19.95 UK: £12.48

- Can you Exploit it?
- How to produce it
- Can you make money?
- Where to get help
- Industrial Design
- Copyright
- Points of caution
- Patent applications
- Sample licensing agreement

- Is the idea original?
- How to distribute it
- Can you protect it?
- A word about patents
- Trademarks
- First steps
- Possible problems
- What are your chances?

99 pages; softcover; ISBN 0-920847-65-X Canada: $24.95
USA: $18.95 UK: £12.48

The Canadian Business Guide to Patents for Inventions and New Products

By: George Rolston

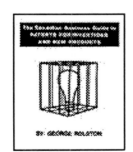

Protect Your Intellectual Property

An International Guide to Patents, Copyrights and Trademarks

By: Hoyt L. Barber & Robert M. Logan

This is your complete reference to patenting around the world. The key elements in the patent process. When to search for earlier patents. When you should file patent applications. The importance of your patent filing date. Understand the critical wording of patent claims. Getting the best out of your patent agent. What the patent office will do for you. What to do if your patent application is rejected. How to go about patenting in foreign countries and how to negotiate a licence agreement. **George Rolston,** is a barrister and solicitor who has specialized in patents for over 30 years.

202 pages; ISBN 0-920847-13-7: Softcover: Canada: $48.00

An abundance of information on step-by-step procedures to obtain exclusive protection for unique ideas, inventions, names, identifying marks, or artistic, literary, musical, photographic or cinematographic works.

Hoyt Barber is an executive with extensive experience intellectual property protection. Robert Logan is practicing U.S. attorney.

305 pages, softcover, ISBN 1-896210-95-3 Canada: $59.95
USA: $44.95 UK: £29.98

You can obtain further information online at:
Canadian Web site: *http://www.productivepublications.ca*
American Web site: *http://www.productivepublications.com*
Order online or complete the order form at the end of this catalogue

Your Homebased Business Plan

-Also-

Working With Your Banker

By: Donald Lunny

Work from Your Home Office as an Independent Contractor:

A Complete Guide to Getting Started

By: Chantelle Sauer

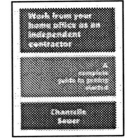

SECTION I - The Business Plan for Homebased Business: a step-by-step guide to writing your plan.

SECTION II - Working with your Banker: the fundamentals of borrowing and how they affect you.

Donald Lunny: an entrepreneur and consultant with many years experience in organizing and restructuring companies.

52 pages; softcover; ISBN 0-920847-35-8   Canada: $14.95
USA: $11.95   UK: £7.48

An independent contractor is someone who works from his or her home or home office e.g., consultants, entrepreneurs, business owners, freelancers and outsourcers. Learn about the advantages and disadvantages as well as the legal obligations. Also get many ideas on how to become an independent contractor.

Author, **Chantelle Sauer**, has spent four years as an independent contractor. She knows from first-hand experience how to get work.

166 pages; Softcover; ISBN 1-55270-077-1: Canada: $24.95

How to Buy or Sell a Business

Questions You Should Ask and How to Get the Best Price

By: Don Lunny

Evaluating Franchise Opportunities

By: Don Lunny

The decision to buy or sell a business requires careful consideration. It may affect the course of the participants future lives. Yet a surprising number of owners rush into transactions without adequate preparation. Find out how to set the price, locate prospects, evaluate offers, close deals and finance purchases.

Author, **Donald Lunny**, has many years of business experience and has been involved with the purchase and sale of many businesses.

134 pages, ISBN 1-896210-98-8 Softcover Canada: $24.95
USA: $18.95 UK: £12.48

Although the success rate for franchisee-owned businesses is better than for many other start-up businesses, success is not guaranteed. Don't be "pressured" into a franchise that is not right for you. Investigate your options. Find out how to evaluate the business, the franchisor, the franchise package, and yourself.

Author and business consultant, **Don Lunny**, shows you how to avoid the pitfalls before you make a franchise investment.

75 pages; softcover; ISBN 0-920847-64-1 Canada: $19.95
USA: $14.95   UK: £9.98

You can obtain further information online at:
Canadian Web site: *http://www.productivepublications.ca*
American Web site: *http://www.productivepublications.com*
Order online or complete the order form at the end of this catalogue

Page 8

Steps to Starting and Running a Successful Business in CANADA

By: Don Lunny

Managing your own business can be a rewarding experience but survival can be tough in today's economy. This book shows you the essential steps to ensure that your business is profitable.

Author, **Don Lunny**, is an experienced business owner and consultant with many years of experience.

190 pages; ISBN 0-920847-85-4; Softcover   Canada $34.95

Checklist for Going into Business

By: Don Lunny

Points to create your own profitable business if this is your dream. Starting it is reality. But, there is a gap between your dream and reality - that can only be filled with careful planning. You need a plan to avoid pitfalls, to achieve your goals and make profits. This guide helps you prepare a comprehensive business plan and determine if your idea is feasible.

Don Lunny is an experienced business owner and consultant with many years of experience.

53 pages; ISBN 0-920847-86-2; softcover: Canada: $19.95 USA: $14.95   UK: £9.98

Tips for Entrepreneurs

How to meet the challenges of starting and managing your own business

By: Henry Kyambalesa

This book is the culmination of a 3-year research study into the challenges faced by entrepreneurs when they become their own boss. Tips for those about to start a business & tips for those already in business. Decide whether self-employment is for you. Practical advice on getting started. The skills you will need

Henry Kyambalesa is a tenured lecturer in Business Administration. He holsds B.B.A., M.A., and M.B.A. degrees.

194 pages softcover; ISBN 1-896210-85-6 Canada: $26.95 USA: $19.95   UK: £13.48

MAKE IT ON YOUR OWN!

How to Succeed in Your Own Business

By: Barrie Jackson

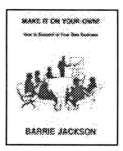

What it takes to run a business and make it succeed. Contains practical, hands-on information, for immediate use. Learn from the author's personal experience and mistakes. Lots of anecdotes from the author's business adventures which make for interesting reading with a "practical punch"

Before his untimely death, **BARRIE JACKSON**, forged Cooper Boating Centre into Canada's largest yacht charter company.

212 pgs, ISBN 1-896210-37-6; Softcover;   Canada: $29.95 USA: $21.95   UK: £14.98

You can obtain further information online at:
Canadian Web site: *http://www.productivepublications.ca*
American Web site: *http://www.productivepublications.com*
Order online or complete the order form at the end of this catalogue

**Business Planning
and Finances**

**Confederation College
Entrepreneurship Series**

**Business Relationships –
Development and
Maintenance**

**Confederation College
Entrepreneurship Series**

Business Planning and Finances takes a pragmatic and hands-on approach to business planning and financial management, and is written in straightforward language free of technical jargon. It includes a thorough review of the role of planning, the benefits to be realized from planning, and the use of a plan as a management aid.

174 pages, ISBN: 1-55270-091-7 Softcover   Canada: $34.95
USA: $25.95   UK: £17.48

The success of any business hinges on the effective management of three critical categories of business relationships. These are a firm's relationships with its customers, with its employees, and with the individuals and organizations that supply it with essential goods and services.

78 pages, ISBN: 1-55270-093-3, Softcover   Canada: $19.95
USA: $14.95   UK: £9.98

**How to Write a Million Dollar
Adventure Novel**

**Novel Writing as a
Profitable Profession**

By: Dr. Ray Mesluk

**Software for Small
Business
2001 Edition**

**A review of the latest
Windows programs to
help you improve
business
efficiency and productivity**

By: Iain Williamson

A structured approach to writing your novel quickly and easily. Master the techniques of novel writing and turn them into a profitable career.

304 pages, ISBN 1-55270-001-1 softcover Canada: $34.95
USA: $25.95   UK: £17.48

For new and experienced users. Covers operating systems, word processing, desktop publishing, voice dictation, graphics, video, photos, spreadsheets, accounting, databases, contact management, communications, Internet software, security and virus protection.

345 pages, softcover; ISBN 1-55270-082-8   Canada: $39.95
USA: $29.95   UK: £19.98

**You can obtain further information online at:
Canadian Web site: *http://www.productivepublications.ca*
American Web site: *http://www.productivepublications.com*
Order online or complete the order form at the end of this catalogue**

**Entrepreneurship and
Starting a Business**

**Confederation College
Entrepreneurship Series**

Entrepreneurship and Starting a Business provides a comprehensive introduction to entrepreneurs and what they do, and is a must-read for anyone who has aspirations to start and run their own business. The book examines entrepreneurs, their values and behaviour, and factors that contribute to their success and failure. It also takes an in-depth look at how they spot business opportunities or come up with business ideas.

110 pages, ISBN: 1-55270-090-9 Softcover   Canada: $24.95
USA: $18.95   UK: £12.48

Small Business Finance

**Confederation College
Entrepreneurship Series**

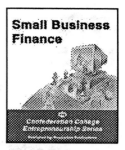

Small Business Finance was designed with the start-up business owner/manager in mind and provides a detailed overview of the organization and operation of a business from a financial perspective. Developed as a combination textbook and workbook, it takes the reader step-by-step through each element of a company's finances from pre-startup costs all the way to record keeping and financial monitoring for an established business.

136 pages, ISBN: 1-55270-092-5 Softcover   Canada: $29.95
USA: $21.95   UK: £14.98

Youth Entrepreneurship

**Confederation College
Entrepreneurship Series**

Some of North America's most successful businesses have been started by people between the ages of 15 and 25. If you are a young person with a business idea or a desire to start your own business then this informative and practical book should be a must-read for you. Learn from the experiences of others and improve your prospects for success.

108 pages, ISBN: 1-55270-094-1 Softcover   Canada: $24.95
USA: $18.95   UK: £12.48

**The Entrepreneur
and the Business Idea**

**Confederation College
Entrepreneurship Series**

If you ever wondered what entrepreneurs are like; where they look for business ideas and opportunities, and what kinds of thinking and tools some of them use in their approach to a possible business start-up, then this introductory book should prove very helpful to you. It includes both a self-assessment and a business opportunity assessment tool, and advocates a "damage control approach" to getting into business.

50 pages, ISBN: 1-55270-089-5 Softcover   Canada: $14.95
USA: $10.95   UK: £7.48

**You can obtain further information online at:
Canadian Web site: *http://www.productivepublications.ca*
American Web site: *http://www.productivepublications.com*
Order online or complete the order form at the end of this catalogue**

Anybody Can Sell!

Sales Strategies to Increase Your Business Profits

By: Don Varner

The Basics for Sales Success

An Essential Guide for New Sales Representatives, Entrepreneurs and Business People

By: Bill Sobye

Written for those who have started a business and have limited selling experience.

- Covers creative marketing and sales presentations.
- Hints on self-motivation and how to handle rejection.
- Discusses different kinds of buyers and how to handle them.

102 pages; ISBN 1-55270-004-6; Softcover Canada: $18.95
USA: $14.95   UK: £9.48

An introductory book which covers the basic points on how to:

- Find customers
- Dress for success
- Set goals
- Success and rejection
- Study your prospects
- Handle "the butterflies"
- How to include humour
- Business versus pleasure

Bill Sobye has 28 years of experience as a Sales Manager.

157 pages; Softcover; ISBN 1-896210-65-1   Canada: $24.95
USA: $18.95   UK: £12.48

MEETING THE SAMURAI

Two Hundred Power Strategies for Doing Business in Japan

By: Jonathan King

Reach the Global Marketplace

A Canadian Guide to Researching Foreign Markets and Online Sources

By: Richard B. McEachin

Author, **Jonathan King**, learned the language and worked in Japan for six years as a business consultant and director to two Japanese "Fortune 500" companies. In this book he shows you how to export your products to the heart of Asia's largest, yet toughest economic market.

119 pages, softcover, ISBN 1-896210-40-6   Canada: $19.95
USA: $14.95   UK: £9.98

Advice on hiring an outside researcher. Shows you what is available online and in print. Written for both the newcomer and the experienced exporter. Author, **Richard B. McEachin**, is an expert with over 20 years experience in gathering and analyzing intelligence material.

193 pages; ISBN 0-920847-92-7; softcover Canada: $24.95

You can obtain further information online at:
Canadian Web site: *http://www.productivepublications.ca*
American Web site: *http://www.productivepublications.com*
Order online or complete the order form at the end of this catalogue

Marketing for Beginners

How to Get Your Products into the Hands of Consumers

By: Iain Williamson

Covers the basics of marketing for new entrepreneurs. How to make people aware of your products. How to get them to buy. How to get products into the hands of consumers. Traditional channels of distribution versus direct marketing. One-on-one marketing versus mass marketing. A look at the Internet as a marketing tool. Ways to promote and advertise your products. After-sales service and the lifetime value of your customers. Sources of marketing information. The author has been marketing products for 20 years.

215 pages, Softcover, ISBN 1-896210-97-X   Canada: $29.95   USA: $21.95   UK: £14.98

Marketing Beyond 2000

Why you will have to use the Internet to market your goods or services in the 21st. Century

By: Iain Williamson

The Internet will become an awesome marketing tool in the 21st. Century. Learn how its current limitations are being overcome. Take a look at the future of radio, TV and newspapers. Glimpse at the marketplace of the future. The author says it's up to you to take advantage of this tremendous marketing tool. Find out how!

194 pages, ISBN 1-896210-66-X; softcover Canada: $27.95   USA: 21.95   UK: £13.98

Selling by Mail Order and Independence

By: Donald Lunny

Your step-by-step guide to seeking independence with your own mail order business. Also invaluable, if you are an established business owner who wants to add a mail order department or to purchase an existing mail order business. Learn the essentials from

Donald Lunny, who is a business consultant with over 25 years experience in sales, marketing and promotion in Canada.

109 pages; Softcover; ISBN 0-920847-24-2   Canada: $16.95   USA: 12.95   UK: £8.48

Successful Direct Mail Marketing in Canada

A Step-by-Step Guide to Selling Your Products or Services Through the Mail

By: Iain Williamson

Techniques to Make Money in the Highly Competitive Direct Mail Market. Direct mail as an inexpensive way to reach customers. Ways to keep your costs to a minimum. How to save on postage by using bulk rates. How to get the most out of your computer.

The author has over 15 years experience selling by direct mail.

114 pages, softcover; ISBN 1-896210-39-2; Canada: $19.95

You can obtain further information online at:
Canadian Web site: *http://www.productivepublications.ca*
American Web site: *http://www.productivepublications.com*
Order online or complete the order form at the end of this catalogue

Secrets of Successful Advertising and Promotion

Practical Steps to Growing Your Business

By: Don Varner

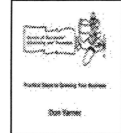

- Covers all the basics of advertising and promoting for business.
- How to prospect for more customers.
- How to increase the average size of your sales.

Author, **Don Varner**, is an expert with many years of experience in this area.

158 pages; Softcover; ISBN 1-55270-002-X Canada: $24.95 USA: $18.95   UK: £12.48

How to Deliver Excellent Customer Service

A Step-by-Step Guide for Every Business

By: Julie Olley

A pre-designed workbook approach for businesses that wish to develop, implement, analyse and follow-up customer service projects. Step-by-step "HOW TO:" ideas and sample formats are included The suggestions can be implemented over time.

Author, **Julie Olley,** was formerly National Manager of Quality Assurance with a major international travel organization. She has designed several curricula for The Canadian School of Management and International Business.

160 pages, Softcover; ISBN 1-55270-045-3 Canada: $26.95 USA: $19.95   UK: £13.48

Jump Start Your New Employees

Get the Most Out of New Hires From Their First Day on the Job!

By: Julie Olley

An organizational tool for various employee transitions with suggested steps to boost initial productivity of new employees from their first day on the job; to minimize the impact on your customers and identify training needs. Also, to professionally handle departing employees while maintaining security and company property. How employee transitions can be used to create a positive impact on your customers.

64 pages, softcover; ISBN 1-55270-084-4 Canada: $12.95 USA: $9.95   UK: £6.48

The Canadian Business Owners Guide to Salary Administration

Entrepreneurial Business Consultants of Canada

Salary Administration Program provides the means or management to:

- Properly analyse and evaluate positions.
- Provide equitable and competitive remuneration.
- Appraise individual performance in the position.

164 pages; ISBN 0-920847-11-0; softcover   Canada: $39.95

You can obtain further information online at:
Canadian Web site: *http://www.productivepublications.ca*
American Web site: *http://www.productivepublications.com*
Order online or complete the order form at the end of this catalogue

**An Introduction
to Personal Computers**

**What You Need to Know
to Get Up and Running**

By: Stephen Belaire

This book will get you from where you are now in computer knowledge, to where you absolutely should be, in the straightest line possible. It will not take a major commitment of your time to get through this book.

Stephen Belaire, has held different positions in the Information Systems field and lives and breathes computers. He is a college instructor who teaches people how to use them.

140 pages., Softcover; ISBN 1-55270-078-X   Canada: $29.95
USA: $21.95   UK: £14.98

**Welcome to the Fun World
of Computers–Become a
"Geek" in No Time!
Neat Things You Can Do
When You Buy a Computer**

by Thomas P. Bun

When the uninitiated bystander encounters the personal computer for the first time, a primordial fear often arises. "This looks really complicated. I may need a Ph.D. before I can take a first step with this." Nothing could be farther from the truth. These pages show that you can start with great ease, and in a short time a large number of useful activities may be carried out with its aid, while spending time in a most agreeable and enjoyable way.

80 pages, ISBN: 1-55270-120-4 Softcover   Canada: $19.95
USA: $14.95   UK: £9.98

THE ONLINE WORLD

**How to Profit from the
Information Superhighway**

**By: Mike Weaver
and Odd de Presno**

This book will change the way you learn, find a job, get information & do business. By the year 2000, the Internet will have one billion users. Can you afford to ignore this market?

Odd de Presno, from Norway, is a consultant and **Mike Weaver**, from Saskatchewan, is winner of the Saskatchewan Association for Computers in Education/Apple Teacher Award of Excellence.

302 pages, softcover; ISBN 0-920847-89-7   Canada: $39.95
USA: $29.95   UK: £19.98

THE NET EFFECT

**Will the Internet be a
Panacea or Curse for
Business and Society
in the Next Ten Years?**

By: Iain Williamson

Are you ready for the greatest change to business & society since the Industrial Revolution? Examine the world ten years from now when entire sectors of the economy may be eliminated and others will be born. Find out who will be the winners and losers and how it will affect you. Prepare for the dramatic changes that are coming!

244 pages, softcover, ISBN 1-896210-38-4;   Canada: $29.95

**You can obtain further information online at:
Canadian Web site:** *http://www.productivepublications.ca*
American Web site: *http://www.productivepublications.com*
Order online or complete the order form at the end of this catalogue

Accounting Software for Small Business

A Complete Review Based on the Results of a Survey by 1850 Accounting Professionals Who Evaluated 1000 Key Features (Year 2000/2001 - Canadian Edition)

Targeted at the over 900,000 small and home businesses in Canada to assist in the selection of the most appropriate software. The survey is divided into three sections. The first rates ten factors: stability, performance, flexibility. ease of use, feature set, reporting, integration with Microsoft Office, e-commerce, third party software and technical support. The second section rates the software by module and the third section contains general comments. Edited by **Alan Salmon**, seminar leader and expert in accounting software.

322 pages, ISBN 1-55270-052-6; softcover; Year 2000/2001 - Canadian Edition   Canada: $134.95

Install Your Own E-Commerce Server for Your Home Or Business

An Inexpensive Way to Start Your Own Online Business With Easy Step-by-Step Instructions on How to Get Up and Running

By: Don Artman

Based on Microsoft® NT Server 4.0 and a cable modem, this book shows you how to start your own inexpensive e-commerce site. If you already own a Pentium® computer, Don Artman will show you how to do it for under $1,000 (US).

Just as Henry Ford brought the inexpensive automobile to the people, **Don Artman** brings you an affordable e-commerce solution. His book is full of straightforward, step-by-step instructions on how to do it.

248 pages; Softcover; ISBN 1-55270-083-6: Canada: $39.95 USA: $29.05 UK: £19.98

Are You Ready for Information Warfare?

Security for Personal Computers, Networks and Telecommunication Systems

Gregory J. Petrakis, Ph.D.

This book is an antidote against hackers and information theft. Access to data is so easy to obtain and it can be stolen or modified. Informational infrastructures can also be destroyed. This book shows you how to counter-attack. The author is an Adjunct Professor at the University of Missouri-Kansas City.

206 pages, softcover; ISBN 1-896210-94-5;   Canada: $34.95 USA: $26.95   UK: £17.48

Learn UNIX in Fifteen Days

by: Dwight Baer and Paul Davidson

This book was written out of the need for a text which presented the material which was actually taught and tested in a typical UNIX course at the college level. It is not intended to replace a comprehensive UNIX manual, but for most students who have not yet spent five years learning all the "eccentricities" of the UNIX Operating System, it will present all they need to know (and more!) in order to use and support a UNIX system.

176 pages, ISBN: 1-55270-087-9 Softcover   Canada: $34.95 USA: $26.95   UK: £17.48

You can obtain further information online at:
Canadian Web site: *http://www.productivepublications.ca*
American Web site: *http://www.productivepublications.com*
Order online or complete the order form at the end of this catalogue

Critical Analysis in Decision-Making:

Conventional and "Outside the Box" Approaches to Developing Solutions to Today's Business Challenges

by: James Briggs

This book examines why some people to make good business decisions more effectively, more often, than others. Great leaders in the public service, business, and the non-profit sectors, remind us that an effective decision-making process is the key to solving problems for any organization. Effective organizations search for leaders who have good problem solving skills.

234 pages, ISBN: 1-55270-116-6 Softcover   Canada:$39.95
USA: $29.95   UK: £19.98

THE LEAN OFFICE

How to Use Just-in-Time Techniques to Streamline Your Office

By: Jim Thompson

This book is for everyone who works in an office. Find out how to foster and nurture employee involvement and put excitement back into continuous improvement. Get the tools needed to improve office productivity. Most importantly, reduce employee stress and frustration, while improving productivity. Find out how this happens <u>with</u> employees, not <u>to</u> employees!

Jim Thompson is a lean production consultant who studied these systems first-hand while with GM and Toyota in California.

138 pages, softcover, ISBN 1-896210-41-4 Canada: $24.95
USA: $19.95 UK:£12.48

LEAN PRODUCTION

How to Use the Highly Effective Japanese Concept of Kaizen to Improve Your Efficiency

By: Jim Thompson

Learn specific techniques and behaviours to improve your effectiveness. Find out about a system that has been used very effectively at the organizational level for over forty years.

Author, **Jim Thompson** has held senior management positions with General Motors and the Walker Manufacturing Company.

146 pages, softcover, ISBN 1-896210-42-2; Canada: $24.95
USA: $19.95   UK: £12.48

LEAN PRODUCTION FOR THE OFFICE

Common Sense Ideas To Help Your Office Continuously Improve

By: Jim Thompson

More ideas for everyone who works in an office:

Be idea-driven	Reduce frustration
Add value	Let others benchmark you

How to use employees' creativity and ingenuity. Employees' feelings **do** count. Author, **Jim Thompson,** is the guru of applying lean production to the office environment.

136 pages, softcover, ISBN 1-55270-025-9 Canada: $24.95
USA: $19.95   UK: £12.48

You can obtain further information online at:
Canadian Web site: *http://www.productivepublications.ca*
American Web site: *http://www.productivepublications.com*
Order online or complete the order form at the end of this catalogue

**Project Management:
Welcome Opportunity
or Awesome Burden?**

by: Robert G. Edwards

This concise, how-to, self-help guide will help both aspiring and practicing project managers. Its content was developed during the author's forty-four years in professional engineering and project management. The principles and practices that he describes are based on his personal experience and can easily be applied to most simple or complex projects.

170 pages, ISBN: 1-55270-086-0 Soft.cover, Canada: $26.95 USA: $20.95 UK: £13.48

Effective Management:

**Interpersonal Skills that
Will Help You Earn
the Respect and
Commitment of Employees**

By: Dave Day Ph.D.

Ten key interpersonal skills for the manager... from choosing a leadership style to the day of completing annual performance evaluations. Contains practical suggestions to increase the productivity and commitment of all employees. Essential reading for all new managers and a resource for existing managers.

Dave Day has over 35 years experience as a manager, consultant and Professor of Management at Columbia College.

182 pages, ISBN 1-896210-99-6; Softcover Canada: $27.95 USA: $21.95 UK: £13.98

**Cooperative Time
Management
Get more done and
have more fun!**

**Chance Massaro &
Katheryn Allen-Katz**

Cntains the wisdom of the last fifty years of research and writing about time management together with my eighteen years working in organizations helping people get the most satisfying results. It is intended for people who want to have goals and want to achieve them. It is interactive and easy to use.The authors are time management experts. Follow the steps which they outline in this 226 page workbook and YOUR RESULTS WILL BE REMARKABLE!

224 pages, softcover; ISBN 1-896210-86-4; Canada: $34.95 USA: $25.95 UK: £17.48

Leadership with Panache

**52 Ways to Set Yourself
Apart as a
Dynamic Manager**

By: Jeff Jernigan

This book cuts to the underbelly of leadership in the modern organization. Divided into 52 "Ways" so that you can select one topic each week of the year for group discussion with your management and supervisory associates. Poses hard hitting questions for consideration.

Author, **Jeff Jernigan**, has over 25-years experience as an organizational development specialist providing companies support in creating, continuing and capitalizing on change. He is the recipient of numerous industry awards.

180 pages Softcover ISBN 1-55270-081-X Canada: $29.95 USA: $21.95 UK: £12.48

**You can obtain further information online at:
Canadian Web site: *http://www.productivepublications.ca*
American Web site: *http://www.productivepublications.com*
Order online or complete the order form at the end of this catalogue**

Market Overseas with Canadian Government Help

By: Don Lunny

Finding Overseas Buyers
Meeting New Customers
Displaying Products Abroad
Conducting Market Research
Government Assistance
Export and Import Permits
Reading to Find Markets
Other helpful sources

Export Questionnaire
Distributors Questionnaire
Export Costing/Pricing
Goods and Services Tax
Thinking in Global Terms
Start with North America
The Bank and the Exporter
Private Sector Financing

68 p ISBN 0-920847-87-0 softcover Canada: $19.95

Everything I Know About Marketing I Learned from High Priced Call Girls

A Marketing Manual for Everyone Who Sells Themselves for A Living

By: Jerome Shore

This book can be instrumental in the success of people who sell personal services. The audience includes lawyers, accountants, consultants, wellness therapistss and others. The marketing skills that make call girls successful are the same as those needed by anyone who sells experience and know-how.

Author, **Jerome Shore**, has been involved with advertising for over twenty years and holds an MBA.

202 pages; Softcover; ISBN 1-55270-054-2
Canada: $27.95   USA: $21.95   UK: £13.98

Speak with Confidence NOW!

A Simple, Unique Program Designed to Make You a Confident, Effective, Dynamic Speaker Every Day, in Every Situation!

By Steve Ryan

Surveys show that speaking in public is our greatest fear. Top-rated radio host and training expert, Steve Ryan, shows you how to make presentations using dynamic speech. Conquer nervousness, improve your breathing habits and enunciation. Learn to avoid vocal mistakes. How to project yourself and use vocabulary and body language advantageously.

Author, **Steve Ryan** hosts the top-rated *KILO/Colorado Springs Morning Show*. He has been in radio for over 16 years.

168 pages Softcover;   ISBN : 1-896210-62-7 Canada: $24.95
USA: $18.95   UK: £12.48

Enthusiasm Pays!

How to Use it Effectively in Your Business

By: Don Varner

People love enthusiasm!

Learn how to use it effectively in your business:

- How to evoke favourable responses.
- Enthusiasm is a high paid quality.
- Five steps to your success.

54 pages, ISBN 1-55270-003-8; Softcover Canada: $14.95
USA: $11.95   UK: £7.48

**You can obtain further information online at:
Canadian Web site: *http://www.productivepublications.ca*
American Web site: *http://www.productivepublications.com*
Order online or complete the order form at the end of this catalogue**

Money Management

A First Course

By: H.J. Fluke

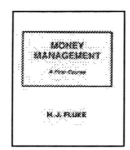

A textbook that demystifies the wealth building process and guides young readers through a wide range of business topics while teaching the principles of personal financial management. Part I covers economics; Part II covers economics from the business viewpoint; Part III covers personal financial planning; Part IV deals with entering the workforce and Part V covers economic activity between nations. Written by **H.J. Fluke,** a business teacher.

136 pages; Softcover; ISBN 1-55270-079-8   Canada: $29.95 US: $21.95   UK: £14.98

Let's be Reasonable!

Effective ways to handle difficult people

By: Clive Lilwall

This book will help you deal with the difficult people in your business and personal lives. It discusses numerous reasons for nastiness and offers you many practical solutions.

Clive Lilwall has taught human communications and writing at Durham College for 28 years and shows you effective ways to handle the difficult people in your life.

172 pages; Softcover; ISBN 1-896210-64-3   Canada: $29.95   USA: $21.95   UK: £14.98

The Ontario Business Owners Guide on How to Meet the Challenge of Pay Equity

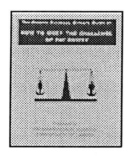

Provides you with a step-by-step guide on how to implement a salary administration scheme that will satisfy the requirements of the Ontario Act. It shows you how to prepare a pay equity plan.

260 pgs; ISBN 0920847-12-9; softcover; price: Canada: $49.95

Market Overseas with Canadian Government Help

By: Don Lunny

Finding Overseas Buyers
Meeting New Customers
Displaying Products Abroad
Conducting Market Research
Government Assistance
Export and Import Permits
Reading to Find Markets
Other helpful sources

Export Questionnaire
Distributors Questionnaire
Export Costing/Pricing
Goods and Services Tax
Thinking in Global Terms
Start with North America
The Bank and the Exporter
Private Sector Financing

68 pages ISBN 0-920847-87-0 softcover Canada: $19.95

You can obtain further information online at:
Canadian Web site: *http://www.productivepublications.ca*
American Web site: *http://www.productivepublications.com*
Order online or complete the order form at the end of this catalogue

The Internet Job Search Guide

By Cathy & Dan Noble

A thorough and comprehensive guide to finding employment opportunities using the Internet. You will learn about resume assistance; career guidance; research and networking. This book takes a step-by-step approach. Contains hundreds of Internet addresses covering a wide spectrum of employment opportunities. This guide will help both first-time users as well as experienced net surfers. It is concise and easy to read.

208 pages; Softcover; ISBN 1-896210-63-5   Canada: $29.95
USA: $21.95   UK: £14.98

HOW TO SELL YOURSELF INTO A JOB

Successful Job Hunting Using Sales and Marketing Know-How

By: Dr. Ray Mesluk

Worried about the difficult questions you might be asked in an interview? Are you focussed on your lack of experience? Do you like to talk about your accomplishments & qualifications? Stop thinking "my failings", "my successes", "me".

Learn from **Dr. Ray Mesluk**, an expert with a Ph.D. in Mathematics who has applied sales and marketing techniques in his job searches. He has worked for a leading recruitment firm.

184 pages; ISBN 0-920847-91-9; softcover Canada: $29.95
USA: $21.95   UK: £14.98

HOW TO GET A JOB!

By: Paul Shearstone

Learn interview fundamentals How to prepare mentally
What makes a good résumé   Types of interviewers
Ways to maintain credibility   Reason for different questions
Master the confident answer   How to turn the tables
How to ask for the job   How to GET THE JOB!

Paul Shearstone is President of Colby Lewis Management Consultants and an experienced recruiter and sales trainer.

Softcover:

English Edition: 54 pages; ISBN 0-920847-36-6
Canada: $14.95 USA: $11.95 UK: £7.48

French\English Bilingual Edition: ISBN 0-920847-37-4
Canada: $24.95 USA: $18.95 £12.48

30 Minutes to a Better Job!

Step-by-Step Instructions for Getting a Better Job Made Easy!

By Don Varner

Applies to any age, any educational level & in any field!
Get a job that makes you happy!

Earn more money!   Create killer résumés!
Free job counseling!   Secrets of interviewing!
Make them want you!   How to land that great job!
Locate over 33,000 jobs & their salaries!
"The only job security in today's society is knowing where the next job is and how to get it!"

52 pages; ISBN 1-896210-89-9 softcover   Canada: $9.95
USA: $7.99   UK: £4.98

You can obtain further information online at:
Canadian Web site: *http://www.productivepublications.ca*
American Web site: *http://www.productivepublications.com*
Order online or complete the order form at the end of this catalogue

SUCCESS is the
Best Revenge:
Gold Medal
Career Management

By: John Stewardson
and Bob Evans

How to Get a
Really Great Job!

A Complete Program
if You Hate Your Job
and Don't Know
How to Go About
Changing It

By Donald L Varner

- A timely book for "The Brave New World" of job searches
- Practical advice to show you how to win at the career game
- Read it if you are employed or are looking for a job

John Stewardson and **Bob Evans**, between them have fifty years experience in human resources, contract operating executives and executive outplacement and career planning.

277 pages, softcover, ISBN 0-920847-88-9;   Canada: $39.95
USA: $29.29   UK: £19.98

This book is written for people at any age; at any educational level;for any field; in any market! If you follow Don Varner's advice, you can watch your happiness and your salary soar... as your job turns into a career!

240 pages; Softcover; ISBN 1-896210-90-2 Canada: $29.95
USA: $21.95   UK: £14.98

A Guerrilla Manual for
the Adult College Student

How to Go to College
(Almost) Full Time in
Your Spare Time... and
Still Have Time to Hold
Down a Job, Raise a
Family, Pay the Bills,
and Have Some Fun!

By: Mike Doolin

Biological Happiness

Nature's Secrets for
Successful Living

By: Claude Maranda, M.D.

This is a "how to" book. It's intentionally short on theory, long on practice. It's full of the mistakes the author and others made and provides advice on how to avoid making them yourself.

Author, **Mike Doolin**, has been there. He will help you develop the personal organization you absolutely must have to get a college education while your life is full of a lot of other responsibilities.

296 pages; Softcover; ISBN 1-55270-048-8   Canada: $34.95
USA: $26.95   UK: £17.48

Happiness is the most significant preoccupation of mankind. This book lets you examine the medical, biological, anthropological and philosophical underpinnings of happiness. The author unmasks religious wishful thinking, spiritual "mumbo-jumbo", and the traditional psycho-babble found in print.

Dr. Maranda is Physician-in-Chief at a Montreal hospital. Learn from him how to increase YOUR state of Happiness.

404 pages; Softcover; ISBN 1-55270-024-0   Canada: $48.95
USA: $36.95   UK: £24.48

You can obtain further information online at:
Canadian Web site: *http://www.productivepublications.ca*
American Web site: *http://www.productivepublications.com*
Order online or complete the order form at the end of this catalogue

Salary Administration

Prepared by:
Entrepreneurial Business
Consultants of Canada

**Take Control
of Your Money**

**Success Starts With the
Opportunity to Plan for
the Rest of Your Life**

(American Edition)

By: Donald J. Davison

Salary Administration Program provides the means for management to:

- Properly analyse and evaluate positions.
- Provide equitable and competitive remuneration.
- Appraise individual performance in the position.

Salary Administration prepared by Entrepreneurial Business Consultants of Canada; 164 pages; ISBN 1-55270-085-2; Softcover; Canada: $39.95 USA: $29.95 UK: £19.98

You have needs and wants. But the way in which you manage your time and money depends on your stage in life (single, married, divorced, working, retired, etc.) together with your value system. It is up to you to take a long look at yourself and decide if you want to control your lifestyle or not. If you do ... then read this book.

Author, **Donald J. Davison**, was a banker who went through a divorce and an earlier-than-planned retirement. These experiences taught him a lot about being a single parent, a senior and a survivor.

Take Control of Your Money by Donald J. Davison: 260 pages; Softcover; ISBN 1-55270-080-1 USA: $29.95

The Old Mission Academy

**A Novel of One Charter
School's Experiences
Implementing
Lean Education**

By: J. K. Thompson

A novel about more learning for less money. It suggests that it is possible to remove the waste from education using lean production business concepts. It also outlines the controversial issues surrounding the establishment of charter schools. The book ties this into the basics of lean production, which is changing the very nature of how the world will be making things in the 21st century.

The Old Mission Academy by J.K. Thompson, 206 pages; ISBN 1-896210-91-0; Softcover USA: $21.95

Salary Administration

Prepared by:
Entrepreneurial Business Consultants of Canada

Salary Administration Program provides the means for management to:

- Properly analyse and evaluate positions.
- Provide equitable and competitive remuneration.
- Appraise individual performance in the position.

164 pages; ISBN 1-55270-085-2; Softcover; Canada: $39.95 USA: $29.95 UK: £19.98

Take Control of Your Money

Success Starts With the Opportunity to Plan for the Rest of Your Life

(American Edition)

By: Donald J. Davison

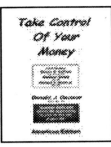

You have needs and wants. But the way in which you manage your time and money depends on your stage in life (single, married, divorced, working, retired, etc.) together with your value system. It is up to you to take a long look at yourself and decide if you want to control your lifestyle or not. If you do ... then read this book.

Author, **Donald J. Davison,** was a banker who went through a divorce and an earlier-than-planned retirement. These experiences taught him a lot about being a single parent, a senior and a survivor.

260 pages; Softcover; ISBN 1-55270-080-1 USA: $29.95

The Old Mission Academy

A Novel of One Charter School's Experiences Implementing Lean Education

By: J. K. Thompson

A novel about more learning for less money. It suggests that it is possible to remove the waste from education using lean production business concepts. It also outlines the controversial issues surrounding the establishment of charter schools. The book ties this into the basics of lean production, which is changing the very nature of how the world will be making things in the 21st century.

206 pages; ISBN 1-896210-91-0; Softcover USA: $21.95

She Delivers Steel

Inspiration from a Grandmother who Drove Her Dream to Reality

By: Patricia Prior

Fulfill your dreams - accomplish your goals both physical and emotional! At age 43, **Patricia Prior** left a successful career in motivational speaking to fulfill her dream of becoming a truck driver. She hauled steel through the Rockies to Vancouver and seven years later she became a grandmother! Her story reflects the true concept of real accomplishment. The journey is rewarding. Read this book and enjoy the trip!

162 pages, softcover; ISBN 1-896210-92-9; Canada: $24.95 USA: $18.95 UK: £12.48

You can obtain further information online at:
Canadian Web site: *http://www.productivepublications.ca*
American Web site: *http://www.productivepublications.com*
Order online or complete the order form at the end of this catalogue

TAX HAVENS FOR CANADIANS

Ingenious Ways to Preserve Your Wealth (and Have Fun Doing It!)

By: Adam Starchild

Are you overtaxed? The offshore solution is your answer. Details on 37 tax havens & what they offer. Tax havens are now within reach of Canada's "middle class". Learn how to save as much as half of your annual taxes. Protect your assets from professional malpractice suits, divorce proceedings, or no-fault liability suits. **Adam Starchild** is the author of many dozen books and articles.

341 pages, softcover; ISBN 1-896210-18-X; Canada: $48.95

Slot Machines: Fun Machines or Tax Machines?

A Technician Reveals the Truth About One-Armed Bandits

By: Ian B. Williams

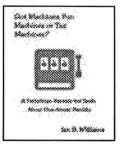

How slot machines work and how to play them. Covers the pay-out systems. Will help you have a better casino experience. Also examines the social implications of slot machines in our society; both the positive and negative.

Ian B. Williams is a certified electronics technician and a trained slot technician, who worked for several years in the casino industry

134 pages; Softcover; ISBN 1-55270-049-6   Canada: $24.95
USA: 19.95   UK: £12.48

STOCK MARKET PANIC!

How to Prosper in the Coming Crash

Dave Skarica

A warning for every mutual fund and stock investor! The sharp sell-off in late August 1998 showed how confidence can erode overnight. How do you avoid watching your wealth evaporate? Find out How to Prosper in the Coming Crash!

228 pages, softcover; ISBN 1-896210-93-7   Canada: $29.95
USA: $24.95   UK: £12.48

Shoplifting, Security, Curtailing Crime - Inside & Out

By: Don Lunny

If you are a shopkeeper or business owner, this practical, hands-on book will alert you to the alarming theft rates you may be exposed to. From petty theft, bad cheques to armed robbery, you get advice on dealing with the situation and how to train staff.

Discusses internal theft by employees - how you can recognize it and how to reduce it. If it alerts you to just one problem, it could pay for itself many, many times over.

115 pages; softcover; ISBN 0-920847-66-8:   Canada: $29.95
USA: $21.95   UK: £14.98

MONEY BACK GUARANTEE

*I understand that if I am not completely satisfied, I may return any book within **100 days** of receipt for a full refund with no questions asked.*

ORDER FORM

Qty.	Title	Price
	ADD Postage: $7.00 first title for USA & Canada UK:£11.20	
	ADD $1.25 Postage per title thereafter USA/Can UK: £1.80	
	SUB-TOTAL	
	ADD 7% GST - Canadian Residents Only (others EXEMPT)	
	TOTAL	

Name_____

Organization_____

Street_____

City/Town_____State/Prov_____ Zip/Postal Code_____

Phone_____Fax_____

☐ Cheque   ☐ VISA   ☐ MasterCard   ☐ American Express
Credit Card Orders: can be faxed to: + (416) 322-7434

Card
Number_____

Expiry Date (Month/Year)_____

Cardholder Signature_____

Mail to: **Productive Publications**
PO Box 7200, Stn. A, Toronto, Ontario M5W 1X8
Phone: (416) 483-0634 Fax: (416) 322-7434

Page 26